Run
Ruby
Run!

**By Ruby Reed Lyons
with Sean David Hobbs**

**Edited by
Anne Teachworth**

To order additional copies of this book, contact:

THE GESTALT INSTITUTE PRESS
1537 METAIRIE ROAD
METAIRIE, LOUISIANA 70005 USA

Phones: 1.800.786.1065 or 504.828.2267
24 Hour Fax: 504.837.2796

Website: www.gestaltinstitutepress.com / www.teachworth.com

E-mail: ateachw@aol.com

CONTENTS

Foreword   i
Editor's Note   iii

SHOOTING
Chapter 1   3
Chapter 2   17
Ruby's x-rays   25
Chapter 3   27

SHOCK
Early Photos   47
Chapter 4   49
Chapter 5   69
Chapter 6   91
Chapter 7   107

CRISIS
Young Adult Photos   133
Chapter 8   135
Chapter 9   157

TRANSFORMATION
Later Photos   183
Chapter 10   185
Chapter 11   199

Basic Principles of Life   213

Foreword

On July 16, 1983, a forty-three year old woman named Ruby Reed Lyons was shot in the face while unloading her groceries at 9 p.m. in front of her home in Uptown New Orleans. Two young thugs got away with her purse, containing only twenty dollars.

This life-changing event and her recovery is the central part of her autobiography. You see, Ruby was told by all her doctors that she would never walk or talk again.

Completely paralyzed on her right side with the bullet still lodged in her left brain to this day, Ruby *has* fought her way back. Through constant physical, mental and emotional therapy, she has learned to walk, talk, write and think again.

The extraordinary resilience of this amazing woman is the focus of this book. Ruby has been an inspiration to hundreds of people, many of whom would have given up if they hadn't witnessed what Ruby has done to make a new life for herself. I'm fortunate enough to be her friend — a friendship, I cherish.

Mary Jane Phelan
New Orleans

Editor's Note

Several years ago, I had the honor of suggesting to Ruby Lyons that she write her story, not just of her survival but of her amazing recovery from a gunshot wound to her face. Here is that story, not just one of survival, but of transformation.

This book, though not written in chronological order, is a collection of Ruby's private thoughts and personal awakenings as she remembers them, some more vividly than others. As you read this story, you will journey with her from the day of the shooting through her long hospital stay to her current state of recovery.

You'll visit with Ruby in her Catholic childhood, relive her carefree college days, her marriage, her children, her divorce, and her brief days as a Social Worker. Travel with her as she enters into a long series of rehabilitation treatments after the shooting, and once more, go back there with her as she wonders how she brought all that suffering on herself.

Weave in and out of all the difficult facets of her life as she wakes up after the shooting unable to talk and gradually learns to speak again — first confined to bed, then getting around in a wheelchair, to walking with a cane and now finally, without one.

Run along with Ruby in her memory as she recalls those blissful morning jogs in the park long ago. Sit with her as she begins to question her unconscious motivation for having asked God to make her "perfect life" difficult. "Be careful what you pray for," she now reminds herself everyday. "God *does* answer your prayers."

From the beginning of this project, I had the title, "Run, Ruby, Run" planted firmly in my mind. You may find many places in this book where you, too, might indeed wish Ruby had run away, or perhaps you'll notice places or people she did run away from or to, or should have, but mostly, you'll anguish with her as she realizes she may never run again.

I say, "may never run again," rather than "never will," because Ruby has already surpassed several "never again" obstacles in her recovery, so who knows, she's likely to do that, too. For Ruby, as you will read, the impossible just takes a little longer. Let's all cheer her on from the sidelines ... *Run, Ruby, Run!*

I am proud to know her and publish her story,
Anne Teachworth, Editor

SHOOTING

Chapter 1

Two weeks shy of my 44th birthday, as I stood by my boyfriend's car, groceries in hand, two teenagers approached me by surprise. It was so dark out, about 9 p.m. None of the other neighbors had their lights on. As I looked up at my house, I wished I had turned some lights on before I left that afternoon.

The teenagers must have been hiding behind the pine tree next to the car because they slid right up next to me when my back was turned. I felt their hands on my purse and I angled the purse away; spinning to face them.

They were both black — men or boys — I don't know — but if they were men, they were acting like boys. They told me to give them my purse. Holding it to my side defiantly, I said "NO!" I remembered I had taken a Judo course twenty years earlier and was sure they weren't going to take *my* bag.

It's still a shock to me that without a moment's hesitation, one of them took out a gun and shot me in the face at point blank range. The bullet went into my nose and sliced into my brain, smashing through two/thirds of my left lobe. In a blinding flash, I was on the ground, laying on my face in the dirty street, blood gurgling out of my nose and onto my blond hair ... and me not even knowing what had happened to get me there. One of them had the nerve to ask me, "Are you alright?"

"Oh, I'm just fine." I nodded, hardly moving my head. Years of proper Southern breeding came up automatically and I managed to say the most polite thing even with the blood gurgling out of my mouth as I spoke.

The teenagers ran off, probably as much in shock at what I had said as at what they had done to me. A neighbor had heard the shot. He ran out of his house to see what was going on. There I was, lying face down in the street. Running back inside, he called 911 and then came back out with a towel. I remember this part, but from then on, the images of that time come and go as I passed out and came back and faded out again.

Suddenly, I am at Baptist Hospital and the nurses are cutting away my clothes. I had been wearing a black jump suit I really liked. The nurses took off my matching black shoes. I wouldn't see those wedges again until five months later when I was back home from Texas Institute for Rehabilitation and Research, or as it was referred to, TIRR. Still covered in my blood, they were laying by my closet door, waiting there to remind of the trauma I had experienced, bringing me right back in time to the events that preceded the shooting.

*

On the day that it happened, I had gone jogging around Audubon Park like I did everyday. I started later than usual because it was a Saturday and I didn't have to go to work at Waldo Burton Boys Home where I was Social Worker. Thinking it was just the

beginning of another ordinary day, I ate breakfast, put on my
tennis shoes and headed out the door. Uptown New Orleans
was where I had lived since I was eighteen and had come from
Beaumont, Texas, to attend Loyola University, a Catholic college
close to the Garden District.

Summers in New Orleans are traditionally hot even at 8 a.m.
But this was July 16th, and the heat had only just begun. Liquid
humidity laid over everyone in our saucer-pan of a city. Back
then in 1983, I always wanted to get away for the summer and
live somewhere else. As a child, my family had spent summers in
Colorado, and as an adult, I had taken my children there to cool off,
too. When I retired, I was going to move to Colorado permanently
... preferably to Boulder, the perfect place for an Uptown Christian
Hippie like me.

*

Meanwhile back at the ranch that fateful day on Webster Street,
as I started to run down the sidewalk on the way to Audubon Park,
three blocks away, one of my son Tom's friends, John, who was
staying at my house wished me well. Back then, everyday I ran five
miles, bouncing along and zazening to myself. Zazen is an Oriental
meditation, similar to the "runner's high."

I passed friends and waved to them. Usually, I ran in the dark at
5:30 a.m. and had gotten in the habit of seeing the same crowd,
but at 8 a.m., it was a different crowd, the "late runners," all of who
were familiar faces to me even though I didn't know their names.

Everything seemed to be going well, at least on the surface ...
no signs of the impending doom that was to come. I was in great
physical shape with five healthy children from ten to twenty

years old, and I was free. Having divorced my ex-husband two years earlier, I already had my own house and my own job. I was set. Currently working at Waldo Burton Boys' Home, I was also volunteering at Hospice and wanted to work full time with them. Given my tragic background in childhood, I had always wanted to help the dying. I was fascinated with that.

*

Something else strange was going on. There was an unfinished place inside of me. Beyond the happy façade of that morning's jog, my deeper self told me something was missing in my perfect life.

I remember thinking I had everything but I still I wanted something more. I had my children and a good boyfriend, but I still felt lonely. Maybe it was that no man was right. I didn't feel complete and I didn't know why. I needed something.

It's hard to say exactly what was missing in my life. Even when I ran, I could feel some lack inside me. The lack of whatever I needed inside to complete me would come through the runner's natural high and worry me enough to keep me from fully appreciating the peaceful look of the world outside. The leaves on the trees and bushes shimmered on the edges of my vision, and the birds flew about making soft circles in the air. Lovely. Lonely.

While I was running, I could be by myself, in deep inside of myself, "on a high" and have "out of body" experiences. In and out, in and out, waving to my friends along the way, I never wanted to miss an opportunity to connect with them or my real inner self.

Comprehending the state of being unfulfilled, I wanted "some unknown something" to fulfill me. At that time, my brain didn't know how to deal with this dilemma, so I did what the psychologists call "a regression." I went back to what I understood to do in childhood and decided to let God solve this problem for me. Let me try to explain.

I believed that suffering was a good thing, meritorious. My mother had suffered through the deaths of four of her children. I admired that in her. There had been no tragedy in my adult life. It's what was missing in my perfect Uptown world.

I wanted to suffer like my good mother had in order to deal with the emptiness I felt inside.

All the Catholic martyrs were heros in my childhood. So I asked God to punish me, to give me pain. I felt this was the only way I could transform into a more advanced soul like my mother. Again and again, I asked God to punish me. Morning after morning, whenever I felt empty, as I ran, I began to whisper through my steady breaths, "Come on Jesus, shit on me."

Can you believe it? I was asking God to make me suffer because that was the way I had been raised to believe God solved people's problems. I was empty and nothing could fulfill me so I decided to let God take over. Be careful what you wish for.

After the morning run, I came home, took a bath and went to visit a Hospice patient who was dying of cancer. For your information, Hospice only deals with the dying process, offering counseling and support to both the patients and their families.

Volunteering with Hospice was a familiar world for me. People
dying was somewhat like being back in my childhood. My perfect
Uptown life seemed boring to this tragedy. Soon I was going to be
working with death full time as a paid employee. I felt at home
there and excited. (Oh, shit!)

The patient I visited that Saturday, July 16th, was a woman who
had cancer and knew she was going to die. Sometimes she accepted
this fact. Other times, she didn't. She had two grown daughters; one
who was mentally unwell and the other, a drug addict, who was
married and good to her. The woman had given of herself all her
life. She had filled up her days with her husband, her children and
her job at a beauty parlor.

Now at the end, she told me she was happy to die because her
husband had died before she had. The woman believed he couldn't
have helped her through this cancer anyhow and his dying first had
saved him from her pain. Now she could rejoin him in heaven.

I stayed silent as I listened to the dying woman. There again was
the emptiness in life which I had felt earlier that very morning
while running. The dying woman felt it, too. There was that
familiar longing from my childhood, a void that could only to be
filled with death.

After helping my Hospice patient, I left and went directly to
Schwegman's Grocery to pick up some food. I had been with the
woman since 3 p.m. and it was now 4, early afternoon.

That evening, I had a date to see my boyfriend, Larry, who lived in
the Faubourg Marigny, an older district of New Orleans, right below

the historic French Quarter. Larry was a cardiologist. He was the kind of man who rarely opened up to anybody but with me he had.

Two years earlier, after the first night we had spent together, Larry had asked me to marry him. Feeling instantly ashamed for some unknown reason at this offer, I looked away and sadly said, "Thank you Larry, but I don't want to get married again. I'm never going to marry again." Any other woman in her right mind would have been thrilled to say "Yes" to him. But I backed away from his offer of a good life together.

After that conversation, we dated on and off, often taking sabbaticals from each other and seeing other people. Even though I didn't want to be with anyone else and wouldn't have sex with the other men I was dating, I think Larry did have sex with the women he dated. (He was a good man but Larry was also a *man*.)

My father had always been my hero, my ideal man. In my childhood, I had not ever known about his affairs. Later, I would find this infidelity out from my husband, who had learned it from my mother and father's servant, Murphy. As the story goes, my mother was pregnant with my sister, Anne, when my father ran away to Mexico with his secretary. I don't know whether he asked her for forgiveness, but when he wanted to come home after Anne was born, my good Catholic mother took him back.

Two years after Anne was born, the next child, named only Baby, died twenty-four hours after being born prematurely. One year later, I was born. When I was one and a half, four-year old Anne drowned in a tragic accident. My earliest memories were filled with tragedy and death.

After dinner that fateful night, I gave Larry my station wagon because he was leaving town the next morning to go bird watching. My station wagon had a luggage rack on the top for his raft. He lent me his Mercedes Benz to use while he was out of town. I drove home with two bags of groceries in the back seat.

It was time to break up with Larry again, I mused. Something was missing. Maybe I was looking for the impossible, I thought. Little did I realize then that finding real love was impossible if I didn't love myself. It was 9 p.m. when I pulled up to my darkened house. Almost everyone on my 800 block of Webster St. was elderly and this was way past their bedtime. Little did I realize then that I was about to meet a horrible fate, and have my wish come true at the same time.

*

My whole family came to see me while I was in Baptist Hospital. All of my children and my ex-husband and Momma and my siblings, Ranny, Peggy and Mary came to see me.

My memory of that time is not entirely clear. I was in and out. I guess days went by without my realizing it ... they did a series of CAT scans and x-rays ... but they couldn't do an MRI back in 1983. They didn't have that technology.

Larry told me later that he had asked me if I wanted to live and I said "Yes," but I don't remember that. I don't remember much from that time.

It was in that first week after being shot that my best friend, Mary Jane, and another close friend, Margie, came to my "bedroom," a private room in the hospital and washed the matted blood off my hair. I told them how happy it made me to have clean hair again. That felt so good.

A week after being shot, I was hit with a stroke. It was slow coming on. People told me I was under close observation for days and yet no one knew it was coming. When the doctors realized I was having a stroke, they put me back in intensive care. People tell me now I was in great pain during the stroke but I don't remember. I was in shock, on all kinds of special medicines and couldn't feel anything.

One bit of pain I do remember is when the nurses tried to put in an IV for nourishment and medication. They stuck my left hand repeatedly trying to find any vein, but they couldn't, so a specialist was called in and immediately found a vein in my right hand.

When the stroke was over, I was totally aphasic (which means an inability to talk) ... I was like a new born baby. But it was more like being dead. And I wanted to be. I couldn't do anything for myself anymore. I not only couldn't talk, I couldn't feed myself, I couldn't walk, I couldn't go to the bathroom. I was utterly dependent on others, on what my caretakers could do for me. I was no longer free and independent. Whether it was Momma, or one of my siblings, or one of my children ... I now had to depend on others entirely.

At Baptist Hospital, I was ashamed. As the time passed and my condition stabilized the doctors put me back in a normal hospital room. Once I could start having visitors, I pretended to be asleep to avoid the feeling I was having. I didn't want to see people at all. I didn't want them to see me and what I had become.

Yet people came in my room all the time and spent the day. I would try to sleep as much as possible in the daytime when people came to visit. If I wasn't sleeping when people visited, I keep my eyes closed and played "possum."

It was at night that I would be wide awake. I just lay there, eyes open and looking at the darkness. There was nothing to do, but I couldn't sleep. During the night, a kind nurse would rub my back. I would lay there and try to find *myself* inside.

I wasn't able to fool everyone with this sleeping game. One day, my therapist, Anne Teachworth, came to see me. At the time she came in, I had several other visitors in the room and was pretending to be asleep. Anne took one look at me and told everyone in the room to leave. Right now! I remember her saying, "OUT ... OUT ... OUT!" to everyone, getting louder as they tried to stay, persisting until all of them had left us alone.

She sat on my bed, touched my hand and said "Ruby?" just once. I stopped pretending and opened my eyes right away. I looked at her. I don't remember what she said next — I was still very confused at that time, and on a lot of medication but she talked to me like I was a person, not a patient. It felt good. I felt like someone understood me. All I could say back to her was "So so," but it meant, "Thank you *so* much." Because she had talked to the me inside, I had found me again and was happy to know Ruby/me was still in here.

My doctor at Baptist Hospital was Ed St. Martin and four weeks after the shooting, he began my rehabilitation. One day, he came into my hospital room and said he wanted to test me. Even though I was in speech and physical therapy by that time, it still hadn't fully dawned on me that I had been shot. Not until much later did I find out I still had a bullet in my brain. I looked at him incredulously.

I still wasn't able to talk to others but now I could talk to myself in my mind even if I couldn't get the words I meant out. "Test me for what? What are you going to test me for?" I didn't know if he knew I really wanted to talk to him but couldn't. The helplessness made me just wanted to run away. But inside was the only place I could run to now. So I started to close my eyes to get away from him.

Before I could, Dr. St Martin continued, "Now, I know you can't talk but I'd like you to show me what these things are for." He took some keys out of his pocket and a fountain pen and set them in front of me on the bed. I took the keys with my left hand and made like I was turning a lock open with them. Then I took the pen and made like I was writing in the air.

"That's real good, Ruby. Real good. I think you're ready to start your rehabilitation. It's time to get you out of this bed." He patted me on the shoulder. I was mute, happy to get out of bed finally, but the only thing I could say was "So-so-so." And so I said "So-so-so" to Dr. St Martin. He nodded, looking down at me sadly and walked out of the room. I couldn't help but notice his sadness.

Later my best friend, Mary Jane, told me that all my doctors at Baptist Hospital had very low hopes for my recovery. They had said to my family and friends, "Don't look for much from Ruby. She will at best be in a wheel chair for the rest of her life. She will never walk or talk again."

No one told me what the doctors were saying at the time, and it was a good thing that I didn't know. Also good, there were no mirrors at Baptist. So I couldn't see myself either. Mary Jane said my face was all swollen and disfigured.

Anyhow, they started my rehabilitation at Baptist Hospital in
New Orleans. They began by putting me upside down in a special
rehabilitation chair. I'm not sure why they did that but I guess it
was a start. I would hang there for a while and then they would
turn me back around. And then they would wheel me back to my
bedroom. There was nothing I could do for myself. And nothing I
could do or say to stop them from doing whatever they wanted to
do to me. The whole right side of my body was like a brick after the
stroke and I couldn't move it.

I was catheterized at Baptist Hospital. It took me almost six weeks
to not need the catheter anymore. They took it out sometime
around the end of my time at Baptist. Then I could use the bedpan.
But only for Number One. Also, I was — how do you put it? Plugged
up with Number Two. I hadn't had a bowel movement in quite a
while. The pain medications they had me on had a side effect of
constipation.

Larry got a friend of his who was a proctologist to come down and
take a look at me. The proctologist turned me over on my side in
the hospital bed and with his hand in a plastic glove cleaned out my
colon. What a blessing! What a saint he was! What a job he has!

The decision was made for me, (not by me) that I would go to
TIRR, The Institute for Rehabilitation and Research, in Houston,
Texas. TIRR was chosen over F. Edward Hebert — a hospital in New
Orleans — because TIRR was near Beaumont, Texas, where my
parents and siblings all lived. The plan was for me to be at TIRR
on the weekdays to receive top notch rehabilitation; then on the
weekends, I was to return to Beaumont and stay with Momma.

My immediate family, my children and close friends all lived in
New Orleans but it was decided that I really didn't have anyone
there to look after me. My children were too young or they were in
college. My ex-husband, Pio, was doing other things. My boyfriend,
Larry, was busy with his career. My close friends could have helped
but it was a lot for me to ask of friends to look after an invalid every
weekend. But I couldn't ask anyone anything anyhow.

I went to Beaumont because Momma and Daddy were still alive
and living there. Though they had recently divorced, it was thought
that since they were all so near, my family could be of more help to
me. Also, most of my siblings were still in Beaumont.

In the end, I guess everyone in New Orleans was just in shock.
While I was in Baptist Hospital, I had my 44th birthday. I remember
it a bit. One of my daughters was there with a cake.

Chapter 2

Being at TIRR was a tough experience. We patients all worked at that hospital. There wasn't a lot of time for me to sit around and pretend I was asleep. It was like we were at boot camp and it had to be that way. No one would have gotten better had they not been so hard on us. At TIRR, they started to get me off the pain medications I had been on since being shot. And my head began to clear.

One big problem that remained was that I could no longer see the way I used to. My left eye was now turned in toward my nose. The bullet had damaged my left optic nerve. It had the overall effect of making me cross-eyed. I could still see out of my left eye but I had to change my posture to do it. Instead of seeing straight ahead like normal people, I had to turn my head and look from the left to see what was in front of me.

Since the bullet had destroyed two-thirds of my brain's left lobe, I was left with partial sense loss on the right side of my body. In terms of sight, I had lost all of the right peripheral vision in either eye. Even today, I can't see anything in my right peripheral of both my eyes. Even if I close my right eye and try to use my left eye to see the right peripheral, I am still blind.

The overall effect of my left eye being crossed and the loss of visual abilities due to the brain damage meant that I couldn't focus on anything. The world had suddenly become two blurry layers. In some of those layers, there were spots of emptiness. At TIRR, they had me cover my right eye one day and my left eye the next. In this way they said, I would begin to learn to see again.

On Tuesday afternoons, the stroke patients would wheel themselves into a small room on the first floor of TIRR. Upon reaching the room, we stroke patients formed the wheelchairs into a semi-circle. The orderlies did not help the patients wheel to the room or form the semi-circle. It was thought that the patients had to do everything on their own.

Since the doctors at Baptist had said I'd had a stroke, I was treated like a stroke patient at TIRR. I was able to move my own wheel chair since the left side of my body worked. After we patients formed the semi-circle, a social worker would come into the room and sit on a chair in the middle of the circle. She was so nondescript. I wouldn't know her if I saw her today.

She began by asking everyone how we were. Since most people couldn't speak or their vocabulary was very limited, there was very little response to the woman's questions. For example, by the time I made it to TIRR, I had relearned how to say "yes" and "no," but under stress, I still reverted back to saying "so-so-so."

The social worker would try to draw us out with questions. Or maybe frustrate us. She was a sort of counselor, asking us questions to help us realize what had happened to us and how we were still human. That was a stretch.

I guess I felt pretty stupid during these sessions but I also felt more comfortable in that room saying, "Yes. No. So-so-so" than I did in the normal world where people could really talk to each other. In that small room, we all were the same and I felt a camaraderie with the disabled people around me. So for that small amount of time, I got to feel like a normal human being.

At TIRR, I began to realize that I was changed forever from the other Ruby.

Change; I had learned in my studies of Philosophy about change. I didn't want to accept this change. For years afterward, I would wake up in the mornings and believe, really believe that everything was still okay with me. Then I would feel my right limbs unmoving and I would remember it wasn't.

Even today, there are mornings that it is hard to get up out of bed. Actually, it is hard to wake up period, knowing that I have to start all over again. Nevertheless, I do manage to get up, praying to the Holy Spirit, praying to the Goddess ... but it is that first little wanting to stay in bed, wanting to stay away from everything that comes regularly. I just want to lay in the fetal position. I don't even think, I just want to lay there in darkness and have everything outside over with and back like it was. Sometimes the prayers don't help me at all. And I'm still there with my eyes closed and the birds outside the window. I don't want to move. But I manage to get up anyhow day after day.

I'll be honest with you — then — at those times, the only thing I feel is a hard anger. I see those two teenagers. I can see their hands but their faces are a blur (like they made mine). They take out the gun. I'm still struggling with them over my purse.

And then bang, there ... it's over. Then I'm on the street, and they are asking me, "Are you alright? Are you alright?"

I will get up then! My eyes are open. Do I like holding my butt in every time I take a step? Do I like my right side being semi-paralyzed because of the stroke? This anger gives me determination — a cement wall — to stand up against everyday.

But I got what I prayed for when I ran in the park the morning I got shot. I prayed, "Come on Jesus, shit on me. I have everything I want." So sure enough, I did it to myself. God took half of everything away, half of my hearing, half of my eyes, half of my smell. And so I deserve this. So I get up anyway.

Sometimes people tell me that I didn't deserve this. But I know I asked for it. I also believe that it had to happen to me. I had to be shot and lose two-thirds of my brain's left hemisphere. I asked for this to happen, my prayers were answered. There are no coincidences.

I look and think of all the people besides me that have been shot and died. And I'm still here for some reason. Maybe it is to write my book and talk to people and tell them to be happy when God sends them a great life. Don't feel guilty and ask for trouble. Don't be ungrateful and rude to God. Say thank you and enjoy.

You know, I'm not the same from this morning till now. You've changed too. From one second to the next, our molecules, our brain synapses are different. There is no constancy. There is no golden realm of security. Things happen and we don't have control over them. But we don't have to ask for trouble either.

Yet we do have some sort of will. That will, best described, is a will to meaning. That was what Dr. Victor Frankel, whom I studied under in Vienna, taught.

After the shooting, I could have gotten fat and sat in that wheelchair for the rest of my life and certainly some people do that. I could still be pretending to be asleep. But I didn't want to be asleep anymore. This was the beginning of my "will to meaning." Volition and involution are the two sides to the same coin. We live with both. Within voluntary choice, there is much which is involuntary and within the involuntary, there is much which is voluntary.

Before I was shot, when I was still running in the park, my prayers really called out for something difficult to happen to me because I thought I deserved it. At the same time, it was just a feeling of guilt that life was too easy, too perfect, and there were no challenges to struggle through. Hmmm ... I had no idea that I would get shot in answer to a prayer.

I believe that before we are born we know what is going to happen to us but then we forget ... and life is really about the whole process of remembering what our supersoul decided for us before we incarnated. Only a few of us are given to know what were the original karmic decisions we have forgotten and then have to live out once we get in a body.

I rubbed raw a bare patch of hair from the back of my head where I thought the bullet was lodged in my brain. It was a nervous habit I would do trying to feel the bullet inside. In fact, the bullet was really a lot lower than where I rubbed but I was fixated on the shooting as I could remember it and the results of the shooting I tried to erase from my thinking but couldn't. In some way, I wanted to connect with this little piece of metal that had changed my life.

*

At the shower door at TIRR, there were two long lines of people in wheel chairs. The men in wheelchairs lined up on the left and the women on the right. One after another, we went in. There was an aide in the showers to push us and clean us. The aide took off our gowns and took us out of our wheel chairs, putting us on a bench in front of the showers. Then, they hosed us down indiscriminately with warm water and lathered us up.

I felt like I was in a prison movie or on an assembly line; one after another after another. Afterward, they put us back on our wheelchairs and dried us. Then we were sent away. They washed us every night like that. One time, a nurse's aide didn't get the shampoo out of my hair. It was really hard to explain to her with "so-so-so" that I still had it in there. Life without words was a charade. Overall the showers were a dehumanizing experience. Yet that is kind of where we were, we patients. I mean we were human but society didn't really think that we were human anymore. I didn't think I was human there either.

As my head started to clear, I began to understand fully what had happened. All I wanted to do was get better. I felt a demand inside. Both reading and running were the ways that I had gone into myself before the shooting. I told myself that I would be able to run again. Inversely, I also wanted to be able to read again. After all, Reed had been my maiden name.

Every day, before the shooting, I had run, and I had been in great shape. Every day, I had read new books and absorbed new ideas. Even if I hadn't actually put those new ideas into practice in my life, at least, I was moving and active, thoughtful and obviously, brave.

Well, in fact, I really was already afraid before the shooting. Like many people, I was intelligent and articulate. But I wasn't making the most of my life. I was still living with fear and the ego that it creates.

Before the shooting, I had wanted things, and gotten most of them. I had lived the "White Picket Fence American Dream." I had the handsome husband, the big house, the family, the money; everything, and it still hadn't been enough. Please don't misunderstand, I'm not saying that all of my life from childhood until I was shot at forty-three was meaningless because it wasn't. My children were wonderful and I learned so much from them. But my life before the shooting was about me always wanting something else ... more ... but I didn't know what.

Now in daily therapy at TIRR, coming off all kinds of medications, I knew exactly what I wanted: I wanted to be able to run again; and I wanted to be able to read again. I would vacillate back and forth between these two goals. They were both first in my mind.

I guess it was a mixed bag of feelings I had. On the one hand, I was very focused on getting better. To that end, I worked hard with the physical rehabilitation people. I also worked on improving my eye sight. Again, I could have felt very sorry for myself and just rolled over into a ball and gotten fat. Some days, I actually thought about doing just that but I was still too vain to get fat.

Consequently, the fact that I had some goals and was working toward them was very important. I think that anyone who goes through a major trauma needs to have a force inside of them which pushes them to do more with their lives than they might have been motivated to accomplish under less challenging circumstances.

Still the real reason I was pushing myself was out of fear and ego. I didn't want to be like my brother, Tommy, who had polio and been confined to a wheelchair from age fifteen on. I thought a lot about Tommy while at TIRR. He had passed away in 1977 and sadly, wasn't there for me after the shooting.

I was afraid of being like Tommy. I was afraid of being thought of as less than human. I wanted everything to be normal, the way I had been before all this. I was in total denial about how I prayed, "Shit on me, Jesus." I didn't know how to process it. It would take years for me to deal with the shooting. But I had been put on a path or rather placed myself on that path. Unbeknownst to me, my supplication to God while running on the morning of the shooting had changed my life. I wish I hadn't been so unappreciative of all I had.

Now I just wanted to get better and have everything be back the way it used to be (even though it wasn't perfect). The reasons why I was starting to fight to reclaim my life weren't the healthy truest reasons but at least I was fighting. Standing up out of the wheelchair whenever I could, still wearing the patch on my eye, I began to practice reading. At least, I was fighting back. I still had a long way to go.

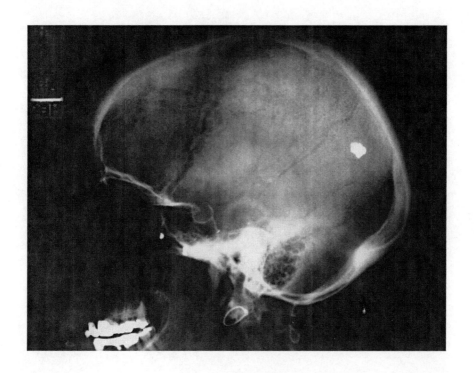

" The bullet went into my nose and sliced through in the brain, smashing the 2/3rds of my left lobe."

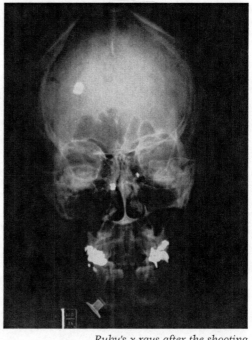

Ruby's x-rays after the shooting

Chapter 3

It was at TIRR that I started having the most vivid memories of my past. I could remember the reflection of the leaves of the pecan tree in our yard, the playhouse, the rope swing, the swing set, throwing pocket knives with my little sister ... all the pieces of my youth came back very vividly to me. I know now that neurologically old memories are the first things to return after a major brain injury. Before the shooting, I remembered my childhood like everyone else but never with the color and vibrancy that my old memories now had.

I wanted very much for my grandparents, my mother's parents, to be there with me. Especially Pa-Pa Phelan, my Grandpa. He was gone now for twenty-five years but I could still remember his affectionate embrace. He would put me on his knee and while saying his rosary, he would pat my back. I was one of the youngest daughters of his only daughter and that made me special. Also, I was the youngest at a time when two of my older siblings had died. Because of all this, Pa-Pa doted on me.

Pa-Pa Phelan (who's real name was John Henry) was a poor, working class Irishman with an education up until the Fifth Grade. He had been raised in North Carolina, one of eleven children. His mother, interestingly, was a German Jew and Pa-Pa Phelan often said in his staccato manner, "I'm a German Jew, a German Jew."

In spite of his half Semitic background, Pa-Pa Phelan was as Catholic as if he had been born and raised in Vatican City.

As a young man, Pa-Pa had moved west to Texas from North Carolina to be a traveling salesman. The story goes that one day he came to Beaumont and was going door-to-door trying to sell scissors. He came to one house and sitting out on the porch was a beautiful young woman rocking in a swing. He asked her name and the girl said, "Johannah" with a Northern accent.

My grandmother, Johannah, who we called "Ma-Mee," was born and raised in Iowa to an Irish Catholic family. That was it. Pa-pa had met the woman he wanted to marry. Though he had no interest in living in Beaumont, Johannah was there visiting her sister, Nellie, and so that was where Pa-Pa ended up.

At that time in early 20th century, Beaumont was growing. The great Spindletop boom was on and everyone had come to get rich on the black gold. The population of Beaumont tripled in a year's time. Everyone was a new Beaumonter and from their efforts, sprung all the great American Oil Companies we know today: Texaco, Mobil, Exxon, and Chevron.

Pa-Pa kept working as a traveling salesman in and around Beaumont until 1913 when he opened a grocery store and began competing with a cross-town Protestant rival, Big Tom Reed. By that time, the oil from Spindletop Hill near Beaumont had all dried up. The town had grown but the Boom was over.

In the early 1900s, Pa-Pa began splitting his time working at the grocery and with a new oil company formed in Beaumont called Yount-Lee Oil. Mr. Miles Franklin Yount believed that though all the oil from the top of Spindletop Hill had been drained if they drilled into the sides of the hill, Yount-Lee Oil Company would find more oil. Mr. Yount needed trusted partners and capital to go into business to look for this oil. Pa-Pa and Mr. Yount were friends and Mr. Yount offered Pa-Pa a share of the new company and the Secretary-Treasurer position if he could come up with some starter money.

Incidentally, all of the business men involved with Yount-Lee were Catholic. So long as you were Catholic — you could be Irish, Italian, or Polish — you were in. Since there were so many Baptists in Texas, we Catholics felt ourselves to be a minority and had to stick together.

Momma told me the story that one day Pa-Pa came home, penniless as usual, having spent all of his money buying supplies to keep the grocery store in business. He said to his wife, Ma-Mee, "Johannah, we've got the chance of a life time. I know you've been saving up. I ask you now to give me all that money, and Jesus willing, with the intercession of all the saints and Mother Mary, we will strike it rich!" Then he made the sign of the cross over his chest.

Now, Ma-Mee Johannah had been saving up. She had $700 hidden away in a cookie jar. Right there, she gave it all to Pa-Pa and he invested the money in the company. A few days after Pa-Pa had invested the money, the new Yount-Lee Oil Company hit "Texas gold" and a second oil boom started! The year was 1925.

The Yount-Lee Oil Company was smart about what they did. They bought up all the land which had been undeveloped on Spindletop Hill and sold it off slowly to the big companies who wanted back into the Spindletop market. In this way, Yount-Lee Oil Company became huge. When the shareholders sold their shares to the big oil companies in 1935, they made more money than any other American business deal prior to that date.

Suffice it to say, Pa-Pa and Ma-Mee were rich. And Pa-Pa became the de facto head of the entire Catholic business community in Texas. He was a wonderful man, remembered not just in Beaumont or in Texas, but all over America and even in Rome as one of the biggest Catholic philanthropists in American history.

He and Ma-Mee built a palace-like mansion in Beaumont and when Pa-Pa died, he left this huge estate to the Catholic Church who made it into a hospital. Pa-Pa was so generous that he would give money to anyone who asked him. Ma-Mee began intercepting his mail to make sure no one had asked him twice for money, fearful he would give all their fortune away.

Pa-Pa and Ma-Mee met with the Pope and got all kinds of honors. Pa-Pa became a Knight of St. Gregory, a Knight of Malta, a Knight in the Order of the Holy Sepulcher, and a Knight of Columbus. All of this didn't come without difficulties however.

Momma told the story of one morning when Pa-Pa and Ma-Mee were coming out of their mansion and saw that some people had put feces and trash on the front entrance. Everyone knew that the KKK had done it. Back in the 1920s and 1930s, the KKK was very powerful in Texas and they hated Catholics as much as they hated black people. I guess after that Pa-Pa got some sort of security guards because trash never appeared on their front steps again.

I really loved Pa-Pa. He would come over for lunch in the middle of a Beaumont summer wearing a full suit and refuse to take off his jacket. Back then, there was no air conditioning. Pa-Pa would ask Momma to cook him some soup. Momma — who couldn't cook to save her life — would make him Campbell's soup from a can and he would shovel it in sweating profusely, talking real quick to Momma with that hooked nose of his, "Real good, Sugar Plum. This soup is real good!"

Pa-Pa also gave the money for the Catholic Church to build St. Anne's Elementary School in Beaumont, a school for Catholic children. This was the school where I and all of my siblings received our elementary education. Since I believe in reincarnation, it is my thought that the Goddess in all of us ordained that the school built with Pa-Pa's funds would be named for the St. Anne who was also the patron saint and namesake of my dead sister, Anne.

But back to Daddy and Momma who met when they were young. Even though, Momma was going to the university, women back then didn't really do much with their education. In fact, when I went off to Loyola University in 1957, Momma told me she had studied the harp while at school in the late 1920s. Nevertheless, "Just go to school and get yourself a man," was her only advice to me.

Daddy was born Randolph Compton Reed in 1910, the Compton coming from his mother Ruby's maiden name. His Momma, Mrs.

Ruby Compton Reed, was my namesake, but we all knew her as Nanny.

Daddy's Daddy, "Big Tom" Reed, came from the Reed clan who were pioneer Texans from around Austin. Daddy's Momma, Nanny, came from the Bertrand-Compton family, a French family who came to North America via San Domingo and Cuba.

The story goes that the Reeds were originally a Scots-Irish family who owned chains of banks and stores in Texas. They were a Protestant, hard-drinking, hard- living bunch of men who ran rough shod over their women. But Nanny straightened Big Tom out and made him live more of a domesticated life. They moved to Beaumont, Texas, where Big Tom opened a grocery-store with his father in 1899. This was the same grocery-store that eventually rivaled Pa-Pa's grocery in the 1920s before he entered the oil field business.

Serendipitously, Momma was born in the same year Daddy was, 1910. And serendipitously, they both fell in love with someone from a rival family years later. But unlike Romeo and Juliet, their union ended the business rivalry between the Phelan and Reed families.

Momma used to tell a story about when she and Daddy went to meet Daddy's kinfolk in Austin. Those Reeds were so audacious! One of Daddy's relatives had the temerity to make advances to Momma when Daddy's back was turned.

In order to marry Momma, Daddy had to become Catholic. That is just the way things were done in the Catholic Church. When they were married, Pa-Pa no longer wanted to be in competition with his new in-laws, so Pa-Pa sold his grocery-store to one of his Phelan relatives.

*

While at "TEAR," as I had come to call TIRR, many friends and family visited me. It was heart-warming that so many people came to see me. Anyone could come at any time during the day but when I had occupational therapy, it took so much concentration, I needed to be alone. You might wonder what occupational therapy is. It is the therapy that teaches me how to think or problem solve. I guess in some ways it is meant to teach me how to do an occupation, thence the name.

I had people coming in everyday anytime they wanted to see me. Sometimes they would come in during my Physical Therapy and other times they would come during my Speech Therapy. Hopefully but rarely, they would come after 4 p.m. when most of our activities were finished for the day.

The people I saw the most were my immediate family: my brother, Ranny, Momma, and my sisters, Mary and Peggy. Daddy came sometimes to TEAR but usually I only saw him on the weekends when I would go with Mary back to Beaumont and stop for a few minutes in front of Daddy's house. We would wait in the car and honk and he would come out and say "Hello" but not invite us in. He'd touch my hair and say stuff like, "How's my little girl?" Then he would go back inside to watch TV or something.

This reminds me of Daddy from years earlier when he would visit my ex-husband and me and our children in New Orleans. He would fly into New Orleans, come to our house, leave the cab meter running to "pay his respects" rather quickly. Daddy didn't even know that his youngest grandson (my youngest son) was a boy until several years after the birth. That was my father. Flat emotions.

Now it was true for me, too. My emotions were flat. I could look out throughout me for miles and miles and all I could see was flatness. Not Texas outside my window. Me. No ups and downs, just an endless line, flat.

Can you see nothing? Well I did. People would come and go and pass through my life. The doctors could put a sling on my arm saying it would help me rehabilitate. I complied. I wanted to get better, so I wore the sling.

But only when Peggy my sister visited, was there a rise in my emotions. She often cried when she saw me. Seeing her cry like that made me lose control and I began crying with her. For those few moments with her, I understood what had happened to me. I was shocked when I saw me through her eyes. I could hardly believe that I had been shot.

While crying with Peggy, I felt somewhat relieved, even though I didn't totally understand why. It was a type of release that happened very quickly every time, and then, I would return to that endless flat emotional state I knew so well. I couldn't feel depression or anger yet, as I said before, because as I now know, I was in shock and couldn't feel things. I just did what was required of me for the moment.

I was actually very lucky that only the lower part of my brain was hit. Had I been hit in the frontal lobe, there is no way I would have been able to make the kind of recovery I have been able to make.

*

As far as I could tell, Daddy had always been a drinker and gambler. He made many serious early mistakes with money but he had a lot of personality and Momma was very much in love with him. So he got away with it. She became resigned to his behavior. Women were raised back then to be subservient and raised with the idea pressed into them that they needed a man for security.

While growing up, I remember Daddy would come home for dinner and pass out drunk into his plate. And we'd all ignore it, like it wasn't happening. We'd pretend that it was normal that his head was in his food! We ignored it because Momma ignored it.

Sometimes, he was so drunk he had to crawl up the back stairway to his and Momma's bedroom. When he finally made it up to the bed, he would pass out. Sometimes, Momma would have me or one of the other kids go and take off his socks while he was out cold. We kids used to hate to do that. We'd hold our noses, remove his socks, toss them in the deepest hamper we could find and then run out of the bedroom gasping while he snored away.

For my entire youth and adolescence, I was in denial about Daddy and his drinking ways. I was his pet, I was Daddy's little girl and he meant the world to me. I was special to him.

I finally figured him out in the summer of 1960. It was right after I had finished college and I was back home for a week before I left to study in Europe for a year (a graduation gift Momma and Daddy were giving me).

Since I had graduated from Tulane University with a degree in psychology, I felt I could somehow fix my parent's relationship. First, I went to Momma and asked her how Daddy could make her happier. She said he could come home on time and not drink so much. Then I made an appointment with Daddy out at his Distribution Company to meet with him to tell him what Momma wanted. I didn't talk about this issue at home with him because I wanted him to take me seriously and what I had to say. Anyhow, we spoke and he said that he would try and do better.

A few weeks later, I left for Europe. While in Europe, I got a letter from Momma saying that Daddy had been stopped by the police for drinking while driving. Daddy knew all the right judges and police so, of course, this ticket was swept under the rug. I realized that Daddy hadn't much cared about our conversation. He was an alcoholic and cared more about drinking than promising.

After that experience, I decided to leave the whole family thing alone and let them all work out their troubles. They didn't. By the time of my shooting in 1983, Momma and Daddy hadn't changed in many, many years. They were finally divorced and after that, were happier after many years apart.

On the weekends, my brother Ranny would drive me to Beaumont and I'd stay with Momma for the weekend. On Sunday, my sister Mary would drive me back to Houston.

When I was with Momma, I felt very at home. She treated me like a queen. Probably because I was suffering like she had over the years. She had that deep sadness which I think began after my sister, "Baby," died in 1938. I identified with her because of her tragedy and she identified with me because of mine.

*

Momma and Daddy's first-born was Ranny, born in 1932. He was followed by their second child, Mary who was born in 1934 and then Tommy born in 1935. Next came Anne, born in 1936. We had a big Catholic family. It was the family pattern. Many children meant success.

In 1938, "Baby" was born prematurely during our family's summer vacation town of Boulder, Colorado. "Baby" was born beautiful, with hair and little tiny fingernails but she was much too early. The doctors had to send to Denver for an incubator but it didn't arrive in time. "Baby" died less than a day after she was born.

Because of this and the pain she felt, Momma wanted another child very soon. In 1939, I was born as a relief from her grief as a replacement baby born to take Momma from the pain she was feeling over "Baby," but tragedy was not over yet.

When I was just over one year old, my family went on an afternoon excursion to the nearby Natchez River. The date was December 1st, 1940. They didn't take infant me along with them. They left me home under the care of Tilly. The story goes that they all drove down to the Natchez River, one of the main rivers which flows from Beaumont to the Gulf of Mexico.

At the outskirts of town, they parked the car on the side of the road, where the road rose up to look at the river. Daddy put the emergency break on and everyone got out of the car except little Anne who wanted to stay in the backseat.

The family crossed the road to the other side and walked up to the river's edge. As they walked, Tommy rode on Daddy's shoulders. Mary and Ranny walked along beside Momma.

At the water, Daddy pointed out at the new marina which was being built, where the new family yacht would be moored. It was a fun Sunday afternoon, a little cold because it was December but on the Gulf Coast, winter can sometimes be very warm.

Everyone was smiling and having a good time. Tommy asked to be let down from Daddy's shoulders and ran around in circles with his arms outstretched, pretending he was a British Spitfire, fighting the Nazi planes over Britain. Mary hummed a song. Ranny turned to look back at his favorite sibling, his little sister, Anne. He hadn't expected to be able to see her but Anne had crawled up to the front seat of the car and she waved at Ranny over the dashboard, smiling at him. Ranny waved back and smiled.

Momma was the first to realize something was amiss. Why was her son waving at the car when Anne had been told to stay in the back seat? If Anne was in the backseat where she was supposed to be, Ranny wouldn't have been able to see her but here he was, waving at her. Momma felt a fear rise inside of her. She jerked around and saw Anne in the driver's seat and Anne's eyes were wide, filled with fear. The car was moving unnaturally, ungodly forward. Everything began to slow down.

Anne had somehow managed to take the car's emergency break off and now the car was rolling, picking up speed. Momma could hear

herself scream. The car was rolling down the road. Then somehow
Anne turned the steering wheel toward the river. The car zipped
over at a right angle onto the land leading up to the river.

Momma ran toward the car, and almost reached it, ready to stop the
car herself with her body. Daddy was right behind her. He threw
Momma out of the way of the oncoming car, breaking both her
ankles as he did. Then he jumped out of the way as the lumbering
station wagon picked up more speed, rolling toward the river's
edge. Daddy called from behind to little Anne, "Jump! Jump out of
the car!"

Anne managed somehow to turn the wheel of the station wagon
again and the car veered between two protective pilings. Had the
car hit one of the pilings, it would have stopped. But the car rolled
past the pilings and to the lip of the river's edge, lifting off into
the air.

Anne opened the driver side door as the car left the ground and
stepped out onto the floorboard. As the car went into the river,
the open driver side door slammed backward with the force of the
water and little Anne's chest was crushed.

Daddy jumped into the river after her. He had just gotten over
pneumonia and so he swam a little slower than he was normally
did. He reached the car as it was sinking and grabbed hold of
Anne's white dress but then the sinking car and current took the
car and jerked the dress out of his grasp. Daddy swam back to
shore, chilled to the bone.

Hours later the police dredged the river looking for Anne and
the car. They called our home when they were found her. Daddy

answered the phone. The police said that they had found the car. Anne's body had been trapped on the front bumper of the car at the bottom of the river.

Later, Momma always would say that, "We were so lucky they found the body. At least, we had something to bury." Afterward, Ranny would walk by the Natchez River, and looking out on it, say, "I will never love somebody like this again."

*

Growing up, my little dead sister, Anne, was a permanent fixture in our lives. There was a big picture of her and her golden locks on the wall in the living room of our house. Momma took pieces of Anne's memorabilia (a lock of hair, a prayer book, a rosary, a baby cup) and put them in a display case on the coffee table in the living room. We used to ask Momma for permission to hold these pieces and she always said let us.

We also used to go to the cemetery on Sundays to visit Anne's grave site and pray. At that time, I would be very careful where I walked because I might be stepping on somebody's grave.

Out of fear for what had happened to my two older sisters, Baby and Anne, Momma wanted very much to protect me, her youngest child, an infant at the time of Anne's death. Momma was also afraid of getting too close to me the way she had with Anne and Baby. The loss of those two children had hurt her so much that she couldn't allow herself to feel too much affection for me, yet she couldn't allow me to get far away either. Momma wanted to put a protective box around me to protect me from dying, too, but not dare to love the Ruby inside the box.

Since Anne had died when I was an infant, I never knew her, and obviously didn't understand Momma's or the rest of the family's response to me, the replacement child. I just felt Momma didn't like me but at the same time was overly aggressive in her nagging need to protect me. This situation and dynamic led me to rebel against Momma when I got older at home. In fact, she often said I was the most argumentative child she ever had. Maybe I was.

*

Momma's and my relationship improved after my brother, Tommy, got polio in 1950. She became more relaxed with me because Tommy took so much of her nurturing over-protective time and his near-fatal illness took her mind off of the death of her two babies.

After being shot, I longed so much to be with Tommy, to try and understand his situation. I felt that Tommy was supposed to be my kindred spirit who would get me through all of my physical troubles. However, Tommy had died in 1977. I could not have him to lean on.

In 1950, when I first learned about Tommy's polio, I tried to cover up how I felt and be tough about things. I would march in a slow way with my friends around the park next to St. Anne's Grammar School during winter. We would chant, "Pol-ee-o. Pol-ee-o. Pol-ee-o." In hindsight, I think this was a coping mechanism to deal with my brother's disease which had taken the use of both his legs, half of his lungs and some of his left arm.

*

The thing was no one in my family expressed any of the emotions caused by death. We looked at death as a blessing on those who received it and a trial for those who were left behind. It was one or the other. But it influenced me and my prayers. It was unfinished business ... unexpressed emotions long to be expressed. Anyway at all. Particularly the deeply repressed ones.

With the help of God, the Son, and the Holy Spirit, we were all on trial all through our lives. We believed that suffering through trials was meritorious. As a family in a Catholic culture, we would say, "Offer it up." We asked saints to intercede and supplicate on our behalves. We believed that suffering and the guilt of penitence allowed us to get closer to God.

But none of this worked! No one was looking at their own emotions! How did we really feel? But how we felt wasn't important.

It was the 1940s. We were expected to be tough. There had been the Great Depression and then the WWII. Few of us knew then how to deal with our anger (many of us still don't). I don't think half of the people in my family even knew what anger was. They just buried it, let it get deeper. As we buried our anger, it got worse. It acted out upon ourselves. As you have seen in my life ... .

People nowadays want to idolize the past but in many ways, we are much freer now. Just because crime rates were lower in the 1940s, didn't mean that people "loved" each other more. In fact, the opposite is true. Back then, everyone knew their place. Whether you were Black or White or a man or a woman; if you came from wealth or poverty or the middle class, you knew your place. Sure, you could change social or economic strata easier in America than most countries, but we still had certain rules which were ineffaceable. And I was raised to follow them. And usually did.

We had pain we had never dealt with. Burying the pain was just a process of fear. We were asleep and fear of waking up is what keeps humans asleep, now and then. It was my family pattern and I followed it automatically and unconsciously.

This was how my people got by. They got by through displacing their anger, but never dealing with their true pain. The church told us to go look for suffering or penance, be it in a monastery or with our families. Hence, we had this ideal of suffering, yet we never really knew how to deal with the pain of personal loss. We stayed brave.

Though we revered Anne, we, as a family, never grieved her death openly. I don't think people faced the truth of our society in the 1940s or 50s. Think of all the boys who came home from the war who had witnessed all kinds of horrors but our society wanted to give them a confetti parade and tell them to forget what they had seen.

A generation later, we couldn't just forget. Society had a lot of problems. We were looking for new answers. When the Beatles went to India, suddenly, many more people were curious about new ways to understand the world. We were reacting against all this buried pain and anger. At least, for a little bit, we were waking up as a society. But ultimately, we can't "wake up as a society," we can only just wake up as a person which is maybe why all these movements from the 60s and 70s didn't work either.

At the end of each week at TIRR, Ranny would pick me up and take me to Momma's house in Beaumont. Momma was always so sad. Things had changed a lot since I was a little girl. After my children were born, Momma and I had gotten over many of our differences. She used to come to my home in New Orleans and spend time with my children and help me.

My becoming a mother totally changed the dynamic between us. She didn't know what exactly to do with me when I was with her on the weekends from TIRR but she could at least finally love me. Momma could love me then, maybe because I didn't die even though I had come so close. We ended up crying together a lot. I needed that contact with her.

When she was dying in 1988, Momma said, "I lost four children before I died — Baby, Anne, Tommy, and Ranny. And almost you, Ruby, when you were shot. I am dying from a broken heart."

SHOCK

Ruby and daddy with her "pow-wow!" dress

Ruby at 5 years old

Ruby at 6 years old

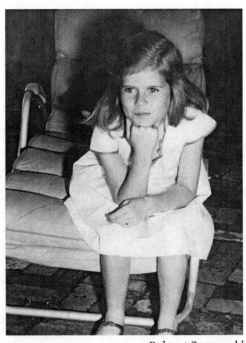

Ruby at 7 years old

Chapter 4

I can still remember the first memory I ever had as a baby. I was sitting in a blue tub looking at the top of the pecan tree out the window, being bathed by a maid, one of Momma's "help." The maid's arms were wet and black. My white arms reached out for her. "There you go. There you go now, little baby."

Ranny was my favorite brother. He had been named after our father, Randolph. Ranny was the oldest of all of us; eight years older than I. He was so smart. He learned Latin, French, and Italian and could speak Cajun French with the help, Beulah and Murphy. He would take encyclopedias with him into the bathroom and read them for close to an hour.

Five of Momma's seven children survived their childhood. Only Anne and Baby died young. Serendipitously, my own five children were born in the same chronological order as I and my surviving siblings had been. It is no coincidence. There are unexplained family patterns that repeat automatically.

My younger sister Peggy and I were very close when we were young. We would sit on a couch in the playroom and Ranny would be our tour leader all over Europe. We especially loved to play with dolls. Our favorite doll was Mary's "Sonya Henie" doll. Ranny used toilet paper and scotch tape to make bosoms for the doll. Somewhat of a future prediction of "boob jobs" ... and Randy's emerging gay nature.

Peggy and I didn't like our other sister, Mary, very much. Mary was seven years older than I and we thought that she always did what Momma wanted her to do.

*

The winter I got back to New Orleans from TIRR was so cold. My children came and stayed with me over the Christmas holidays. They had been staying at their Daddy's house which was just around the corner.

One freezing day in the middle of the holidays, the heating went out in my house and the water in the pipes burst. There was nothing to do until a repairman could come, so I was moved over to my ex-husband Pio's house. I stayed alone in Pio's upstairs bedroom.

One evening, I had to get up to go to the bathroom. I could use a cane to walk small distances by that time and I knew the bathroom was close. The cane I used back then was a four-pronged aluminum cane, the kind of cane used by very handicapped people. It would take another seven months, about a year after I was shot, until I would be able to get around with a normal wooden cane.

Nevertheless, I got out of bed and shakily made my way across the bedroom floor every morning whether I wanted to get up or not. I was so slow. I lumbered along, fearful every minute I would fall over. Not at all stable on my feet, I just dragged my right side lamely along. Of course, I could have just used my wheel chair which was next to the bed but I didn't want to. Using the wheelchair made me think of Tommy and his polio disability and I didn't want to be like that.

Each step was pain. Each movement required my full focus. The bathroom door on the other side of the room seemed very far away. I finally made it to the bathroom and stumbled in, not bothering to close the door after me nor concerned if anyone would pass by and see me on the toilet. In fact, I was hoping someone would.

Back then in the daytime, I would wear a patch over one eye. At night, however, I took the eye patch off. Without the patch covering one of my eyes, my vision became blurred and out of focus. But it was the best I could do dealing with me then, feeling all alone.

One of those nights when I was staying at his house, Pio came into the bedroom. I was in bed about to go to sleep. He lay down next to me. Staring up at the ceiling, Pio asked me, "Why do you think all of this happened, Ruby?" I couldn't respond. Back then, all I could say was "Yes, no, and so-so-so." I could half-way hear, half-way taste and half-way see, but I couldn't say anything all the way.

Actually, I didn't fully comprehend then why it had happened. I had an inkling and didn't want to tell him. I didn't want him to admonish me for praying to God to make trouble happen to me. But I couldn't tell him if I had wanted to and I didn't want to.

When I was a girl, Momma didn't like me much. It was always my fault and she scolded me more than any of her other children. She always admonished me, "Don't be silly Ruby!" It made me want to be more rebellious. But it also made me want to seek a partner who would admonish me like she had. Pio had been a perfect match for that. But he didn't this time. After a few minutes, Pio got up and left. He never was much for words. Now I wasn't either.

Years later, I visited Pio's house and once again stayed in the same room that I had those few days during Christmas 1983. It was amazing how my perspective had changed. The distance seemed so much shorter between the bed and the bathroom. I had conquered both the space around me and the demons within me.

*

I remember Momma had very tight brown pin curls surrounding her head and I thought that if she would just loosen some of those pin curls, she could relax and love me more. The pins must have hurt her scalp, because she was always angry when her hair was up in pin curls. I sucked my thumb until I was eight which isn't normal. I remember they tried everything to get me to stop. Tilly, my nanny, would put steel thumb guards on my hands and still I would find a way to suck my thumb.

Finally, Daddy told me that if I wouldn't suck my thumb for six weeks, he would buy me a bicycle.

Every night, before Peggy and I went to bed (we shared the same room), Daddy would come in to make sure neither of us were sucking our thumbs. I had to start over a few times but finally I was able to make it six whole weeks without sucking my thumb. Daddy gave me a bicycle and just when I was about to ride it, I came down with the measles! While I was in bed with the measles, Daddy put the bike outside my bedroom window so I could stare lovingly down at it.

*

Growing up, I had a crush on Daddy and Murphy. Murphy was a combination chauffeur, downstairs cleaner, yardman, and butler. He lived on the other side of town. Peggy and I used to get Murphy to play "flies and rollers," our favorite baseball game with us. He had the biggest black muscles. He was Creole Cajun. Peggy and I would hang on his arms and he'd swing us round and round.

When he served us supper, Murphy used to play another game. He'd look at me and wink and say, "Ti Du," which meant "Little Ruby" in Cajun French. Then he would serve Peggy and say to her "Ti No," which meant "Little Peggy" in Cajun French (at least, I thought so). He made us feel so special, like we were in on a secret game together. We would giggle. How we loved him!

*

I want to talk about Tilly. Her real name was Viola Clark and she was so wonderful. Everyone called her Vi but when I was a sophomore in high school my boyfriend Tommy said upon meeting her, "Why ma'am you look just like a Tilly!" And we all laughed! From then on, everybody called her Tilly, all my children, my sisters and brothers, everyone.

Tilly came from seafaring people from the Gulf of Mexico, and was actually born on a boat. Her mother died when Tilly was very young and Mr. Clark, Tilly's father, brought Tilly to shore. He took her to a Catholic grocer he knew in Beaumont named Harry Phelan (my grandfather, Pa-Pa) and asked him to take Tilly in since she was just a child. She was a good worker, Mr. Clark said, and she needed a home, not life on a ship.

So as one good Catholic man to another, he asked if Pa-Pa might help him out. Now, I'm a little confused as to why Mr. Clark would go to such a poor man as my grandfather was then for help but everyone knew Pa-Pa had a big heart and was always helping anyone no matter if he had not a cent in his own bank.

Pa-Pa said he would take Tilly and send her to live with Ma-Mee's sister, Anna, in Port Arthur, Texas. Pa-Pa reportedly said, "Let her grow up helping my sister-in-law, Anna, and her husband raise their children. If she does this, she'll always be a part of our family."

Years later, Momma got married to Daddy and Randolph, Jr. or Ranny was born. By that time, Great Aunt Anna had outgrown the need for Tilly, so six weeks after Ranny's birth, Tilly was sent to Momma to help raise her children. She and Momma raised us by the rule that "children should be seen and not heard." We were taught to answer an adult with "Yes, ma'am" or "Yes, sir." As children, my siblings and I had no rights. Thank God, we had loving parents in Daddy and Momma.

Momma and Daddy weren't "yellers." If Daddy was annoyed, he just relaxed, knowing he could go for a drink soon. Momma held in her anger, grinding her molars together, pulling her lips back and away in disgust. For our part, we children were expected not to get angry and not show our tempers. To this day, I still had trouble being angry, even at the boy who put a bullet in my head. That's one reason, I'm writing this book — to get my repressed anger out of my system.

At home, Murphy and Beulah called Momma, "Ms. Reed," and Daddy, "Mr. Reed." Once Beulah and Murphy tried calling Tilly, "Vi," without the "Miss." You should have seen Tilly react!

Some folks said that Tilly was Black, or that her mother or her grandmother had been a Black but Tilly wasn't Black.

In her mind, Tilly was superior to Blacks and any Black who would try to bring her "down to their level" ... well, Tilly showed she was superior. "You will call me Miss Vi!" she said with quiet determination to Murphy and Beulah.

Later on, I saw Daddy talking sternly with Murphy and Beulah in his study. Daddy never raised his voice but you knew when he was displeased. That was the only time I saw Daddy be firm with Beulah and Murphy. They were such loyal servants. Beulah and Murphy never called Tilly, just "Vi" again. It was only "Miss Vi" for the rest of their lives.

I loved Tilly very much. I remember every Tuesday was her afternoon off, and Peggy and I would wait for her to bring us a surprise. Lo and behold, she always brought us Crayolas and coloring books, bubble gum and bubble-blowing soap and sticks. Tilly was so good to us. In fact, when things weren't right between Momma and Daddy, Peggy and I always said we wanted to go live with Tilly. She was like a surrogate mother.

Tilly had great patience and was always sitting in front of a 3´ × 3´ puzzle, figuring it out meticulously. If we ever lost anything Peggy and I would go to Tilly. We knew Tilly could find it because she could find anything.

*

After the holidays, I had one month off before rehabilitation began again. Promptly on February 1st, 1984, Mary Jane's Dream Team went into effect. Comprised of Linda Wessel, Margy Ruli, Evelyn Menge, Boodie Fransen, Grumpy McFarland, Boo Villere, Sister Jane, Father Keller, and Sister Mary Michael O'Shaunessy, it lasted the first half of 1984.

Mary Jane, my best friend, organized this group of our friends to help in my rehabilitation. The plan was for someone to help me with what therapy couldn't do.

For example, the Dream Team helped me relearn math; simple addition and subtraction. They kept me company and played games to keep me occupied. I am so thankful to Mary Jane and the rest of the Dream Team for all they did. My rehabilitation was a slow process but their actions helped buoy my spirit.

During that first year out of TIRR, a family member stayed all the time at the house with me. Usually, it was one of my children or my brother Ranny. I don't know what I would have done without Ranny and my children coming and helping me at the house.

*

One of the more difficult things about rehabilitation was the loss of independence. You do what you are told. You do what you are supposed to.

I want to talk about how it was to lose myself. Firstly, just from a purely medical scientific standpoint, I lost two/thirds of the left hemisphere of my brain. The bullet destroyed that much on its ride to the back of my skull. This was the part of my brain which stored my logic, my memories, my ability to read, do mathematics, and understand the world. The loss of a good portion of my brain meant that all of those abilities were gone.

Basically put, the me or I of existence was cast into doubt. We are — in many ways — just the aggregate of whole of cells and electricity; neurons and synapses. The question of whether or not there is something more to humans than just our bodily mechanics seems to me to be the primary question we are dealing with when we look at the idea of God.

I came eventually to entirely lose both my religious faith and childhood trust in a Christian God and Jesus. With this change in my belief system, came much fear. I began to really understand that the God and Goddess is in me, and came to a new understanding of the concept of energy in my brain and body. The energy of me, that unknowable, indescribable thing, was an energy of a Universal One.

I had no shame until I went to Kathryn Manion's mansion. The Manions were related to the Younts of the Yount-Lee Oil Company. I was about four years old. After spending the night at Kathryn's home, we kids woke up and decided to play doctor in the playroom. So we began to "play doctor." I was the patient on a little ironing board and had just pulled down my pants for Kathryn who as the doctor, was beginning to operate on me. At that moment, a maid who was watching us, walked into the room and gasped. From then on, I never wanted to stay over at my friends' homes again. I was so ashamed.

*

After I had my own children, Momma told me that when I was very young, she had sewn up my pajamas so that I wouldn't play with myself. But I didn't know about masturbation until I was in college.

I think most grown Catholics have some kind of complex about sex. I know my Momma did. I remember Momma trying to tell me about babies. We were both so ashamed, so to her relief and mine, I told her I already knew. Another time, she tried telling me about menstruation. Momma explained how every twenty-eight to thirty days all women bleed. It was a privilege, she said, because only women did this, which meant only we could have babies.

Unfortunately, Momma never told me where on my anatomy the bleeding was to come from so I always checked my naval to be sure I wasn't bleeding there. Later, a friend of mine informed me that you bleed from "down there." We couldn't say "vagina."

*

As a little girl, I used to sit on the front lawn every Friday, waiting for Life magazine to be delivered by the postman. I wanted to beat everyone else to it. Even though I couldn't read, I just loved the pictures. On the cover of one issue was a picture of a woman with a big stomach. I opened the magazine and saw more pictures. One was of a woman with a grotesque expression on her face. She was "having a baby." There were guard rails on her bed. The woman was gripping them. Ever since seeing that picture I wanted to have babies, even though I knew it hurt a lot. I didn't want the pain.

Before I knew about "the birds and the bees," I knew about women having babies. Otherwise, I didn't see why anyone would want to get married. As a girl, the only reason I could see for marriage was so that a woman would have somebody, a man, to help her up and down the stairs to the front door of the hospital when she was pregnant. The main hospital in Beaumont, St. Therese, had a double flight of stairs out front so obviously, I would need help. After helping a woman up the stairs, what other use was there for a man after that? Once she was married, the man could die and the woman could have all the babies she wanted. I'm laughing as I write this now.

*

I had married at twenty-one, and even though I was a virgin until my wedding night, my sister, Peggy, in the convent at the time my first child was born, figured it must have been a "shotgun" wedding because my first child arrived exactly one short of nine months.

Pio and I had been living in Denver as a young couple but I was so lonely, we moved back to New Orleans for the birth of the baby, and stayed with his mother until we found a place of our own, a basement apartment on Neron Place. Over the next ten years, Pio and I had five children. By then, Pio had established himself as an architect and we had bought a house on Eleonore Street and then another on Webster Street close to St. Charles Avenue, where the streetcar line goes through the Garden District.

We were a "good Catholic family" until we divorced after twenty-years of marriage. I was forty-two years old at the time and Pio was forty-five. Incompatibility was the legal reason, but in reality, it was the lack of being able to communicate our feelings to each other. We had gotten so stuck inside our much too traditional mother-father roles we had lost ourselves.

Living on my own for the first time as a single mother, I had
bought a house I loved just a few blocks down Webster Street from
the house we had lived in as a married couple. At the time of the
shooting, Tom, my oldest, was 21 years old and had just come
home from SMU in Dallas that day and was staying at his father's
apartment. Pia, my first daughter, was 20, and was across the lake
with her boyfriend. Johannah, my second daughter, was 18 at
summer school at the University of Colorado at Boulder. Joshua,
five years younger, was 14 and my youngest son, Merrick, was 12 at
the time of the shooting. Both of them had gone to Beaumont for a
vacation to each stay with one of my sisters.

*

One of the more annoying things about my condition after the
shooting was my laughter. It spontaneously erupted. The bullet had
touched on a part of my brain which affected my laughter. I would
break out into giggles and laughter when I meant to be serious or
when I was angry.

If one of my young sons broke something in the house, I would
burst out laughing when really inside I was livid that he had been
throwing a football around the house! Something which any mother
would be angry about would just elicit gleeful snickers from me.
I was no longer perfect like my mother had been. For this, I felt
relief on one hand and remorse on the other.

At first, I didn't have the capacity to say that I was really angry. As
my speech slowly improved over the years, I would be confronted
with a dual problem. If I got angry, I would burst out laughing, and
then in the middle of the laughter, I would manage to say, "No,
really, Father-fuck, I am damn angry!" But I would still be laughing.
Where did that "Father-fuck" come from?

My family and friends would get odd looks on their faces when this would happen. It was hard for other people to understand that language coming from inside me, I was angry. I guess, they just thought I was "kooky" because of the bullet in my brain. My neurologist had told me that cursing was one of the first things that comes back with the returning ability to speak. What a great built-in excuse I had.

Please know that if you see a person with a brain injury and they are laughing at an inappropriate time, inside that person, they are probably screaming because they know they have no way of expressing their anger other than laughing or cursing.

I'm not sure it was there directly following the shooting but as I woke up mentally, little by little, that flat line of existence which I had experienced in "TEAR" began to develop a few bumps.

About a year after the shooting, in the summer of 1984, I began to notice a ringing pulse in the back of my head. It had something to do with the aneurism and the blood vessels around the bullet.

It only came to me at night when I was laying down and everything was quiet around me. It rang in the back of my head and drove me crazy sometimes. After a few years, I got used to the beeping sound and although it would annoy me from time to time, it became a part of my life.

The beeping didn't stop until I had a second stroke in 1995. It came on because I had just walked the New Orleans Crescent City Classic of 6.6 miles, just to know I could do it. I wanted to get back to running. I had run the Classic only once before the shooting and that was because I had wanted to beat Pio, which I did. But out of the four times I had walked it since I had been shot, twice I had made it all the way to the end. This Saturday, I had forced myself beyond my capabilities because now I wanted to beat myself.

For a week and a half after that, I had a terrible headache and my left eye closed involuntarily. My neurologists sent me to Houston and they did an angiogram on me. Amazingly, the blood had already found another route to take in my brain and luckily, I had no sign effects from that stroke except that my left eye became a little more cross-eyed. When the headaches finally went away, my left eye reopened, and I no longer had a pulsating beeping when I lay down.

✳

Father Ben Wren gave a mass at my house after I returned from TIRR. Father Ben was a Jesuit priest who had taught me Zen during the 1970s at Loyola University. He was a renegade from the Catholic priesthood, who later married and left. Nevertheless, he continued to teach at Loyola after his marriage and on onto his death in the early 2000s.

My house was very crowded for the mass. People filled up my front room and went all the way back to the kitchen. Before the homily, Father Ben asked me to read a passage from the gospel. I was very nervous. He stood next to my wheel chair and helped me with the difficult words he wanted me to read from the gospel passage. I still made many mistakes speaking even with him whispering in my ear.

Saying the definite article (the) and the indefinite articles (an, a) was very difficult. I also would mix up different gender objective/

subjective pronouns (He, him; she, her) and possessive pronouns
(hers, his). So for example: even though inside my mind, I could
understand the sentence, "She was a pretty woman," I might read
it or say it like this, "He was pretty woman." Inside though, I knew
what I meant even though you didn't.

In fact, even today I am nervous about speaking in front of
groups of people I don't know. As I have said, back then, the only
words I could easily say were "Yes, No" and "So-so-so." However,
I could use bigger words. For example, if someone whispered
"refrigerator" in my ear, cognitively, I could conceive of what a
refrigerator was and repeat the word right after hearing it. But
in normal conversation, I couldn't get the word up, out from my
throat. I could be at a friend's house and see their new refrigerator
and want to say, "My, what a nice new refrigerator." But the words
were trapped back in my mind.

The stroke I had after the shooting and the brain damage had
given me dysnomia. Dysnomia is like this: I knew what I wanted to
say inside my mind, but sometimes it came out differently.

Daddy owned a farm outside of Beaumont and we always had
farm animals at our house that had become our beloved pets. We
had "Tom" who was also "Tom Turkey," who was somehow served
one Thanksgiving even though no one could bear to partake of his
flesh. We had chickens, who were really lovely smart animals when
you give them a chance, dogs, a descented skunk who belonged to
Mary, and an alligator named "Hessie June," who was an import
from New Orleans.

"Hessie June "came to us as a baby alligator, not bigger than your index finger. Though we tried to tame her, "Hessie June" had a bad temper and as she grew, she used to snap out at us hissing. So we would tease her with a stick. Actually, baby alligators are pretty easy to manage. If you clamp their snouts closed, they are absolutely helpless.

In the fall, for St. Anne Grammar School's All Saints night festival, I brought Hessie June to the school and blocked off a section of our classroom with a wall of white sheets. I would turn off the lights and shine a spot light on "Hessie June." Then I would come out to my classmates and command them as a barker, "COME and See "Hessie JUNE!" The WONDER of the world! For only 5 cents." The kids would go in and see "Hessie" who would hiss at them and they would scream and come running out. They got their money's worth.

I don't know what ever happened to "Hessie." I think she escaped. She might be in the sewers of Beaumont to this day. Of course, now I'd probably have a much harder time holding her mouth closed! Plus, I'd have to watch out for that tail of hers. Those full grown alligators are vicious with their tails!

I had Blue Cross/Blue Shield Health Insurance when I was shot. I was covered under my social work job. The insurance paid for some of my hospitalization following the shooting. By the time I left TIRR and returned to New Orleans, however, the insurance money was used up and I had quite a large debt to TIRR. Fortunately, my grandparents had willed me some money. I was able to pay off the enormous financial TIRR debt over many years mainly because of this trust.

*

Now that I was back in New Orleans, I was left with a new
dilemma. I wanted to begin my outpatient rehabilitation. All of my
friends and family wanted me to begin this as well, but Blue Cross/
Blue Shield had decided to drop me as a client. I guess I cost them
too much money. That's the way insurance companies are.

My sister Peggy spoke to other health insurance companies about
me. All of them said that they would cover me but their policies'
prices were more than it would cost me to just go to a doctor and
pay for their services per session. So Peggy asked Medicaid if the
government would be able to help me pay for my rehabilitation.
The officials at Medicaid said that I had too many assets and that I
would have to sell my house to be able to afford them.

I certainly didn't want to sell the home I lived in and loved. It was
the house I had bought following my divorce and it was home.
So Peggy and I decided that I would pay for the rehabilitation
specialists and doctors out of my own pocket. I was blessed because
I had the financial resources to do this. It wasn't cheap.

All through my life I had felt guilty about the money my family
had. It wasn't until I met Ron Hall, my spiritual teacher that I
learned about reincarnation and I got over my guilt about having
too much. The first time I met him, I had told him I had been shot
in the head, and he replied, "I was, too." We instantly bonded.

The next question you could ask is obvious. What if I hadn't had
my family's money? In America, had I been a poor woman I could
have gotten some help from Medicaid. However, Medicaid is very
limited. We have a great problem in our country. If you don't have

money, you can't get good medical care. That's why I believe that every person has a right to good quality medical care. I don't know how this will be brought about but I believe that variants and options provided by socialized medicine need to be investigated.

*

I can remember my first taste of prejudice. I was about three or four years old and I really liked playing with Birdie Parker's daughter who was my same age. By the way, Birdie Parker was our cook who made the best ice box pie!

Well anyway, one day it had rained and like other coastal towns, Beaumont flooded. Birdie's daughter and I took off our shoes and were just wading in the street puddles when my Momma called out to me from our second floor bathroom window, "Ruby Catherine!" I knew from the tone of Momma's voice that I was doing something wrong.

It was not that I was "playing Doctor," it was that I was playing with a colored person (we were not allowed to call them "Negro" because that could be interpreted as "Nigger" and our family never called Blacks that word). I knew inside of me that I was doing something wrong. I never played with Birdie Parker's daughter again. After a while, Birdie got a job somewhere else and Beulah came from Abbeville, Louisiana and became our cook.

I was prejudiced until I started Loyola University in New Orleans at eighteen years old in 1957. I took a Sociology Class which sent me and four other Loyola students to Xavier University which is a famous African—American school in New Orleans. It was really strange being at Xavier. We were the only five White people there in comparison to hundreds of Blacks. I was in the minority and it was scary.

I met a girl sitting on a park bench at Xavier University. She was really nice. We had a lot in common. We joked around and watched everyone go by. She told me about boys at her school and I told her about boys at mine and we laughed at men and their clumsiness. Then I told her or she told me that we ought to meet up more often. And yes, yes, we would do that. We both agreed. Then we paused. We both looked at each other. Meeting would be impossible. She was colored and I was white. We were both Catholics. We weren't allowed in the same school. She had to sit behind the "Colored Only" signs on street cars and buses, water fountains, and churches.

God was a White God wasn't He, not a Black God? God was male God, but not ever a Goddess. And when and where did we give all the power over to a Him ... and why? Fatherfuck! Fatherfuck! It makes me so damn angry now that I think about it again.

Chapter 5

Daddy owned a farm outside of Beaumont and we would visit it often. Daddy had the farm run with a caretaker named Murphy.

On Tuesdays, Murphy would go out to the farm/ranch in the family's truck. He would come back an hour or two later and we, the children, knew what was coming. We'd all gather up in Peggy's and my bedroom. All of us were up there: Peggy, Ranny, Tommy, Mary and me. We looked down from the bedroom window and could see everything that happened.

Murphy usually had the field hands from the farm with him.

They took some cages out of the back of the truck and brought them over to a stump along the side of the house. Then they unrolled a temporary wire mesh fence around the stump.

Murphy walked over carrying an axe. He reached inside one of the cages and pulled out a pecking chicken. He slapped the writhing chicken down on the stump and in one swift motion, Murphy cut the bird's head off.

The chicken's body dropped down and ran around the wire fence, shooting blood.

We children were fascinated, squealing with laughter, watching the birds and the axe from above. We laughed even though we were a little afraid seeing all of that happen. Murphy would sometimes swivel his powerful neck around and look up at us in the window. Though he couldn't see us because it was daylight, Murphy would wink and point at the window. He knew we were there.

Murphy did this again and again in the hot sunshine, repeating the axe coming down and with it, each new chicken's body running around afterward. When it was over, Murphy and the field hand plucked and gutted the birds and gave the meat to Beulah who wrapped the birds and put them in the refrigerator to be eaten as the week went by. We all loved and respected Murphy so much. He was a real loyal help to our family.

For me, Daddy was everything. I had a crush on him and emulated him. When I lost my baby teeth, Daddy pulled the first one out by tying a string around the tooth and the other end around a doorknob. Then — bam! Daddy slammed the door and out the tooth came. He poked his head around the corner and I started to cry but it didn't really hurt, I was just scared from the door slamming noise. "Oh, Daddy's little girl isn't gonna cry now is she?" he teased. He told me that if I left my tooth at the foot of the bed on the floor that a magical rat would come and get it and leave me a quarter. I believed him and sure enough the next morning, I had a quarter. Daddy was magical himself.

*

Years later, Murphy told my then-husband, Pio, that in 1936, right before Anne had been born, Daddy had run off to Mexico with his secretary. He had stayed down there for a while before he came back to Beaumont telling my mother's mother, Ma-Mee, that he wanted to be back in the family. Ma-Mee told Momma to take him back saying, "We won't ever talk about this again." My pregnant Momma took Daddy back. And I truly believe no one talked about it again until Murphy told Pio.

*

I began my rehabilitation partially because I wanted to and also because my family and friends wanted me to. Dr. Patricia Cook was my neurologist for many years. She was a very good doctor. My family didn't much like her though. Dr. Cook insisted that I come into the examination room alone. I think that since there weren't very many woman doctors back in the 1980s, Dr. Cook felt insecure about other people interfering when she was examining a patient. Maybe she just didn't want a lot of people around me like Anne had said years ago when she was trying to talk to the 'real me' in the hospital room.

Dr. Cook checked my eyes and my reflexes. She told me that the first words to return after my kind of brain injury would probably be curse words. And shit, was she right! As my speech improved over those first few years, I would burst out in the midst of my laughing spells, sometimes announcing "Father-fuck!" I'd shout "shit," "cunt," and "fuck" emphatically ... without thinking. This inappropriate behavior went on for about fifteen years. Of course, it got better as the years went by. Finally, in the late 1990s, I got total control and stopped shouting curse words.

As a girl, my family went to Boulder, Colorado, every summer. It was my favorite place to go. Momma and Daddy had a house there and Pa-Pa and Ma-Mee had a house next door.

We'd usually leave Beaumont in late May or early June. Ma-Mee and her two sisters, Nellie and Annie, would drive up with Enoch, the chauffeur. My male siblings (Ranny and Tommy) would accompany them and report back to us by telephone that Ma-Mee and our great-aunts would make them clean the corners of the house's rooms with an orange wood stick.

Pa-Pa had been taking his family up to Boulder since 1917. Back then Pa-Pa was a penniless owner of a grocery in Beaumont.

Ma-Mee had bad allergies so Pa-Pa decided to take her and his family away from Beaumont for the entire summer when her allergies got really bad. The first year they left Boulder, Pa-Pa took Ma-Mee and Momma and Momma's brothers, Uncle Bus and Uncle Mickie, (back when they were little) to California by train. Pa-Pa had heard California was a good place to stop allergies. When they got to California, someone told them that it was better to go to Boulder, Colorado in order to combat allergies. So the whole family got back on a train and went to Boulder. And it really was much better for Ma-Mee's allergies than California had been.

Since Pa-Pa was "penniless," I'm not sure how he was able to take his entire family every summer to Colorado for three months but I guess he scrimped and saved all year to help alleviate his wife's allergies. Anyhow, they stayed in Chautauqua Park, a mountainous park on the outskirts of Boulder. They were able to be entertained, have cookouts, and go for long evening walks.

Chautauqua Park had its own post office, cafeteria and an area for
school teacher summer conventions.

Back then, Chautauqua was mainly populated by female school
teachers coming for teaching workshops in the summer. The
teachers would mostly stay in tents.

After years of annual visits to Colorado, Pa-Pa decided to build
a summer residence in Chautauqua Park, obviously no longer
"penniless." Years later, when I started going to Chautauqua, the
convention/workshop area had been converted into a movie house.

*

Peggy, Mary, Momma, Tilly and I would regularly go up to Boulder
with Pa-Pa. We'd take a train to Houston and from there, we'd take
a fast Zephyr train to Dallas/Fort Worth. In Dallas, we'd get on an
overnight train to Denver. During the war, we'd bring dress boxes
of sandwiches so we wouldn't have to fight for food at the diner car
on the overnight train. Peggy and I rode on Pa-Pa's lap watching the
flat Texas countryside drift by.

One time on the fast Zephyr train to Dallas, Pa-Pa was sitting in
the lounge car reading the paper. Peggy and I were playing around
his feet with toys. The train was going along pretty fast and
someone outside shot at the lounge car right were Pa-Pa was sitting.
The bullet would have hit him in the head but the window was
double-paned and the second pane of glass stopped the bullet. I
guess a hunter must have been out hunting and accidentally hit
the train and almost killed Pa-Pa. Good thing there was a second
pane of glass.

Anyhow, we'd wake up in the morning and there would be the mountains! What a fresh smell! It was so different from the hot South. The air was usually very cold and the water coming out of the faucets was also very cold and very clean. After a train switch in Denver. we'd get on a little bitty train which didn't have air conditioning or anything, just wide open windows. One year, we saw a beautiful golden pheasant almost on the tracks as we rolled by. Peggy pointed it out to me, and I squealed with excitement!

I can still smell that air! Oh, and the mountains. They pointed up and the height shocked us as kids. It was amazing that the land could twist and rise in cliffs. Back in Beaumont, the horizon was flat and vast as a big pancake, just one long line.

But in the Rockies, the world was pointy and the sky was jagged and broken and cool. Oh Boulder! You could sing and run and laugh all day. It was wonderful and it made my heart race every year that we had a chance to go there and experience it. The only bad part was the Philip's Milk of Magnesia Momma made us all drink to readjust our bodies to the mountain clime. Goddess, I hated that taste.

It must have been the summer of 1945 because that year Daddy volunteered for the War even though he was already 35 years old. Since he had experience sailing our family yacht in the Gulf, the Navy made Daddy a Lieutenant and sent him off to Los Angeles for training.

We were in Boulder that summer as usual with Pa-Pa and Ma-Mee. During the war, America really used a socialist economy. It didn't matter if you were rich or poor, everyone was rationed and everyone felt the pain. During the Depression, (I'm too young to remember it but I was told) class differences mattered in how much food you got to eat. But the war changed all that. We were in the fight together and we'd win it or lose it together. There was no question you had to do your part.

It was also advantageous for women. They got to have the men's roles for a bit of time. (Of course, my Momma's generation went right back inside the home after the men came back from Europe and Asia). Not quite women's lib, but a precursor.

I remember the day we won the war. Momma got us kids into the car. Everyone was jumping around happy. We drove down the rocky mountain road to town and Ranny, Tommy, Mary, Peggy, and I took turns ringing a loud old cow bell all the way down! There would be no more blackouts in Beaumont and along the Gulf Coast to protect from the threat of German U-boats. We were safe. We had won.

*

Besides working with my friends on Mary Jane's Dream Team, I began working with a few other specialists. I needed to relearn what I had known with the right side of my brain. So the logic side of my brain was "recalibrated." I could never have done it without my optometrist, Dr. Joyce Adema.

I met Dr. Adema through a nun named Sister Jane.

Sister Jane was the principal at a New Orleans Catholic Grammar school. Sister Jane had met Dr. Adema because Dr. Adema had gone to Sister Jane's school to test the children's eye sight. Sister Jane told Dr. Adema about my shooting and Dr. Adema was curious, thinking maybe she could help me.

My best friend Mary Jane was a good friend of Sister Jane's so through Sister Jane, Mary Jane and I went to see Dr. Adema. I rolled myself into Dr. Adema's office in my wheel chair. By that time — early 1984 — I was starting to get good at using my wheel chair. I had to push the wheel with my left hand which meant that the wheelchair naturally inclined to the left. Since I was always moving, my left foot's job was to push the chair straight. The left foot also was my brake. Dr. Adema examined at my eyes and then tested my vision using letters and numbers at a distance. I couldn't speak the letters or the numbers that I saw. The only thing I could do was write them in the air.

After our first meeting, Dr. Adema made me special prismed glasses. In this way, I was able to see better. Right after the shooting, my vision was very blurred. I was seeing in twos and there were points where I had blindness in my vision. The new prismed glasses cleared up some of these problems. My vision became clearer, but not perfect. I still saw in twos.

I never regained my right peripheral vision but I could see and focus on one thing instead of everything being hazy and in twos.

By being able to see normally again, I could begin to learn to read. Once my brain's synapses had rerouted to be able to read, all the other physical therapies began to kick in. As my brain learned new ways to read, it also learned new ways to walk, to hear, to organize with logic, to speak, and to remember.

I notice a direct correlation between my ability to read and my ability to speak. They both seemed tied to each other. As the years went by and I could read better, so could I speak better.

In this way, the logic abilities of my brain's left hemisphere slowly recalibrated in another part of my brain.

You know, we only use ten percent of our brain's capacities. So for me to lose the use of thirty-five percent of my brain in milliseconds was obviously a huge shock. Yet, our brains have a way of healing themselves. With the proper support and rehabilitation, my brain — my "me" — began to reform and regrow.

To say that my logic is perfectly fixed twenty-five years after the shooting would be a lie. Of course, I still have many troubles with logic. Counting is a daily problem as is the ordered events of life. The direct proofs of science and philosophy are very difficult for me to explain. Directions are also hard for me to give.

Still the improvements in my thought and capacity after the shooting are truly impressive. Because of my dysnomia, there are still times when I have to guess for the word I want to say. Everyday, I learn more. Everyday I grow.

Seeing in ones would take until 1988 when Dr. Adema said I was ready for cosmetic surgery. This surgery would straighten my eye. Dr. Adema arranged for a surgeon to operate and straighten my left eye. After the surgery, using my special prismed glasses, I could see everything as one. Wow! It was amazing to have semi-normal vision after five years.

Following the surgery, I decided I no longer needed vision therapy. I stopped going to Dr. Adema for about two years.

Then when I went back for a check-up, Dr. Adema saw that I was starting to lose sight in my left eye. She said I might go blind in my left eye if I didn't return to doing vision therapy.

After having regained my sight, the possibility of losing it again was very frightening. If I had lost sight in my left eye, it would be like a dumb eye, a glass eye. I didn't want that at all.

So I went back to doing my daily eye exercises. I have been doing them consistently now since 1990. I think they make me smarter as I use more of my brain synapses to solve the exercises. Also, I haven't lost sight in my left eye.

*

Peggy and I shared a bedroom as young girls. In my own home with my family I was safe. At night, I could hear Peggy's little breath from across our room. The memory of her soft breathing brings back childhood dreams and shadows on the wall.

Peggy and I played with flashlights at night, chasing each other's light beams. Each member of our Phelan family (of which Momma was a part) had a flash light. Peggy would hold hers and I would hold mine and in our separate beds, we would try to "catch" each other's light beams. She would shine hers over at mine, trying to catch my light beam when it was motionless. I would try to do the same to her. If one of us "caught" the other person's light beam, the catcher would get a point. In this way, Peggy and I played games until late.

When the clock radio first came out, Peggy and I got one before most other people in town because Daddy was the President of

Beaumont's Philco Distribution Company. He got the radios direct from the manufacturer and gave them to us for our birthdays.

On Fridays, Tilly would take Peggy and me to The Toddle House for dinner and since we couldn't eat meat on Fridays, we'd order hash browns. Fridays, especially for Catholics, are holy days. It is the day Jesus sacrificed himself for our sins. No good Catholic before Vatican II would eat meat on Fridays.

Back then, every mass was in Latin all around the world. It was a very austere language, a special holy language. All of the readings from the Bible and the Gospel were done in Latin. It was only during the Homily on Sunday that the priest would speak in the vernacular to his parishioners. The priest looked up at the Crucifix during the Liturgy of the Eucharist. When he consecrated the offering, the wine became Jesus' blood and the bread became His body, but we never saw the priest's face, only his back. The priest presented this offering up to the Lord and the Lord through the Holy Spirit sanctified our offering. In this way he, the priest, was our anointed representative and conduit with God. We were the priest's flock and he righteously guided us in all things.

Following Vatican II, the church has become common, too populist in its outlook. It has lost the notion that at one time, all the altars of the church were, in reality, holy! The church has lost the realization that there was once a space provided for all Catholics where transformation of the soul occurred and was supposed to occur every Sunday, and every mass.

I was raised with this notion of a living, breathing full Catholic Church. I loved the mystery of our faith. I loved the passion with which priests and nuns and emboldened lay people loved their

God. The incense, the unified language and the Gregorian chants made the church one warm family from Chile to Texas, from Venice to the Congo, everywhere. The church has lost that now. It started to lose it after 1965. The church lost me, too, but that was years later when I realized certain Catholic dogmas didn't work for me.

Yet, now we have the Catholics who are aware and transcend their dogmatic beginning to touch the real God/Goddess in themselves. These are people with whom I can always relate. I believe rare, awake souls realize we are all Gods and Goddesses.

One does not have to be a Catholic to attain this understanding. Any Christian, Muslim, Jew, Hindu, Buddhist, Polytheist, Agnostic, Atheist, or Nihilist, any human, can find a quiet place inside of his/herself and become very aware and very awake. When we are at that awake place, all of the meanings and the ideologies fade, melt off.

Until we get there, we are just our beliefs and childhoods and fears. Upon getting angry, we women, especially women who were born before the full effect of the feminist movement could be felt in American society, cry when we should be yelling. As everyone knows, "Girls are made of sugar and spice and everything nice." This is bullshit; patent bullshit.

But that is how the women in my family were raised. Boys were free, they could do a lot, but we women, no, no, no, no. We had to stay at home, love and support our man and our family. When I started university I would wryly speak of certain girls who were obviously out to get their "MRS degree" at school. But that is what Momma wanted me to do. Everyone wanted me to get married or go into the convent. These were the options I was presented with in life. I wanted something more, I was always imagining what it would be. But I wasn't able to be it until after I was shot.

*

Peggy, Tilly and I would sit in Peggy's and my bedroom and listen to the 1940s radio shows on Friday nights after getting our hash browns. Listening to the radio transformed us.

The three of us with three plates of chocolate ice box pie would huddle around one of our radios and listen to The Fat Man, Ozzie and Harriet, and The Lone Ranger. I remember we used to make the chocolate ice box pie last until 9:00 p.m.

I don't know how I managed not to eat it all because I have the biggest mouth in the world. In fact, I can get my whole fist in my mouth and close it more or less. That is my favorite trick! I was happy for my maiden last name, Lyons, because it made sense for my big "lion's mouth."

While listening to the radio, the world was enhanced. Typical people we knew became murderers and detectives in radio noir. We could see that avenger of evil riding his horse across the long Western horizon.

Whenever we had the chance, Peggy and I would listen to our radios. At night, Momma came in to our bedroom to say our prayers with us. We had to kiss Momma good night.

After she left the room, Momma would check up on us from time to time putting her ear to the door to make sure we weren't listening to our radios. I would say to Peggy, "Good night, Peg." And she would say to me, "Good night, Ruby." just so Momma thought we were asleep. Then when we were sure Momma was gone to bed, we would turn on our radios next to our beds and listen with the volume turned on low.

*

I wanted to stand up and walk and use my right side again. I wanted to walk and run again. Now that I can walk without a cane, I want to run again, too. To help me begin on these goals, I went to a physical therapist named Nicky Schmidt. In working with me, Nicky applied what she knew of the Bobath concept. The Bobath concept (or Neuro-developmental Treatment Approach as it is known in North America) is a way to help physically disabled people. Especially, it is used with children who have cerebral palsy and with adults who have experienced a stroke.

Nicky was really a task master. She made me work hard. She never wanted me to use the wheelchair or the cane. At first, I was compelled to use my four-pronged cane and wheelchair, but as time went by, Nicky insisted that I do everything on my own.

Nicky taught me how to hold my body so that I could walk easier. I had to tuck my butt in and tighten my stomach. If I held them in place, it was easier for me to move my right leg forward. Also, Nicky taught me to keep my joints loose and bent slightly. This way, I had more control over my right leg as I advanced it forward.

We also worked together so that I could gain more movement and control in my right side. As my functional abilities improved, I gained more mobility from my right side. Even though today, I am still partially paralyzed, I can do pretty much everything.

By the end of 1984, I had gotten good enough that I rarely needed my wheelchair to get around. I also didn't need the big metal four-pronged handicapped cane. I just used a little wooden cane. Of course, she didn't like me using the wooden cane either. Because of this, Nicky made me start walking without using the wooden cane. I would carry the cane in my right hand and try to force my right arm to relax at my side. In this way, my right arm gained flexibility and my right hand got better at gripping things.

For about twelve years Nicky and I continued to work together. We practiced walking up and down curbs, stairs, on grass and walking on the street. I learned so much from Nicky. She was worth the world to me. She drove me on and gave me focus. She never let me quit. I am forever grateful to her.

*

When I was five, at night I would go to my bed and "he" was waiting for me. I knew he was under my bed. He dripped buggers. He was The Boogey Man … .

Every night, upon entering my room, I knew that I had to get over to my bed by the count of 10 … or else! The Boogey Man waited under my bed with a black soul. He waited there for me every night. I could see his shining eyes from below the bed. He was curled up in the fetal position down there. He was tall with long fingers and long toes. His hair was unkempt. Across his body, were wrinkles and pock-marked skin. His eyes were perverted. His mouth was in a permanent scowl.

Well, this is what I imagined. I never really got a good look under the bed at The Boogey Man because I was too scared. I would run,

run so fast just to get into my bed before the count of 10 was up and he would come out and grab me.

The Boogey man was everything that was evil. I was petrified of him. In my mind, I invented the reality that if he came out from under the bed, he would attack me; I would become enslaved by him or worse. I would suffer greatly at his hands, and the only end result could be my death. Once or twice, I got all the way up to a count of 7, but I was always in bed by the count of 10. The Boogey Man never got me.

During the day at grammar school, I showed a façade of strength to my fellow classmates. I guess they thought I was something special because I didn't appear to be afraid of anything. I was one of the "cool" kids. As long as the kids in school thought I was just like them and didn't play with dolls, I was considered "tough." They respected me. I felt like I could be anything at school. I was playing a game. What they couldn't see was that I was very afraid of going anywhere, being anything. I wanted protection, and I wanted to feel safe.

My speech therapist was Virginia Dare Rufin. She was my therapist through 1984. Twice a week, she would come to my house. She had a couple of exercises. Sometimes, I would sing with her, other times we would do writing and speaking exercises. We also practiced English syntax. Virginia taught me ways to deal with my dysnomia. If I didn't remember a word, she told me to try to say another word which was similar to the initial word I wanted to say.

Virginia's efforts coupled with those of Dr. Cook and Dr. Adema helped improve my speech considerably. A few years after the shooting, I could be understood, more or less. It was around that time that I began to realize I no longer liked large parties. When I was around a large group of people, I felt self-conscious and nervous. I wanted everyone to understand me, wanted them all to relate with me the same way they had before the shooting. But that could never be. I much preferred one-on-one conversation. In this way, I could get used to what someone was saying to me, and they could get used to how I spoke.

*

The way I really completed my speech rehabilitation wasn't with Virginia or Dr. Cook or Dr. Adema. It was with Bill Cahill.

I had known Bill years earlier but I got to know him well in 1990 and 1991. We saw each other in a mall and said "Hello" and he called me that night, asking me out to a New Years party.

I was shocked. Before the shooting, men had come up to me and occasionally asked me out. But ever since the shooting, it was as if I was untouchable. No man had shown any romantic interest in me since 1983.

So Bill and I went out. And we had a good time. I liked him. We started seeing each other regularly. He was also divorced. We became serious and once we began having sex, I felt a closeness to him that I hadn't experienced to any man since before the shooting. My body was waking up in the intimacy. I felt comfortable opening up to Bill and speaking with him for long periods of time.

Since the shooting, I hadn't experienced such availability in another human being. Mary Jane, my best friend, was always around but she wasn't available enough for constant speech practice. My children were around but they were active in school and new jobs and new relationships. They naturally didn't have time to sit and speak with me for long periods.

Though people could understand me, rarely could I have a long running conversation. But Bill changed all that. We began to speak to each other for hours and hours.

After a few months of dating, we decided to go to Europe during the summer of 1991. For three weeks and three days, we were together constantly. What Bill gave me was an open ear. We talked about everything during that trip. I felt free to say whatever I wanted. After that trip, I was basically where I am today in terms of my speech ability. Those difficult sounds, "an, a, the," had returned. I was talking more normal.

Today, I still have some problems with differentiating between gender-based pronouns (he, him, his and she, her, hers). Also, I still have dysnomia. Not every word I want to say, can I say. I guess my abilities come and go. Oftentimes, it depends on how tired I am. But overall, my speech has generally returned.

It is funny for me now as I age. I begin to see my friends are having the same issues with memory and speech that I had after my shooting. Now I can smile and commiserate with them. They are beginning to see how it feels.

*

Tommy was four years older than me. I never knew exactly what was on his mind but I do remember him looking at me and giggling, holding out his already powerful legs at the age of fifteen. "Look how beautiful and strong they are," he would say. "They're not bird legs like yours, Ruby." Tommy made fun of my legs a lot. "Bird Legs" actually became my nickname and to this day, it still fits.

As a child, Tommy was strong and powerful. In a way, he would have been the masculine man our older brother, Ranny, never was. Ranny wasn't effeminate but he wasn't brawny either.

Tommy loved all sports. In the summers in Boulder, he used to be the overnight cook on all overnight hikes in Chautauqua Park. In the summer of 1950, he came home earlier than the rest of the family because he had to be in Beaumont for St. Anthony's High School football practice.

After Tommy left, all we heard was that Tommy and Daddy were doing fine back in Beaumont. Of course, we didn't talk much on the phone in those days because long distance was very expensive. We came back to Texas in early September and we found that Tommy had a fever. He couldn't do much for a few days. He just lay around the house sick. No one thought this was unusual until one morning Tommy couldn't stand up. His legs just wouldn't move. We were all up in Momma and Daddy's bedroom. The doctor was next to the side of the bed, holding Tommy's limp arm. Tommy's face was red and sweaty. The doctor said a virus was in him and his body had made the fever to push it out.

We didn't know what was wrong but we knew it was serious. The doctor took Tommy's pulse and temperature. Tommy's half boy/ half man face looked up at Momma and Daddy. He was so scared that he was frozen in silence. The doctor said, "I'm going to have to do a spinal-tap. It'll be best to remove the children from the room." We children went outside and stood in the hallway. Mary took Peggy down the hall and they sat together by the stairway. I looked up at Ranny. He was eighteen now and in a week, he was to go off to college at Catholic University in Washington, D.C. There was no look on Ranny's face, just blank composure.

After a few minutes, we could hear Momma crying in the room. Then an ambulance came to the house. Daddy and the doctor hurriedly exited the bedroom to answer the front door and then led two men with a stretcher between them up to the bedroom. As one of the paramedics passed Ranny and me, he said to the doctor, "Galveston has specialists with an iron lung. Let's take him there."

Tommy was loaded on the stretcher and carried downstairs to the ambulance. "It's polio," Ranny said quietly as they took Tommy out of the room. Tommy couldn't hear Ranny but I could. The whole family went downstairs, following the men with the stretcher. I stood in the hallway. I was alone. They were going to hook Tommy up to an iron lung! He didn't have the muscular strength to breathe anymore. The virus was infecting his body, killing the nerves which moved his muscles. Those powerful beautiful legs were now sticks. That young barreled-chest could hardly take a breath anymore.

I bent down on my knees and prayed to God to make my brother stronger. I bowed my head as I said the word "Jesus." You always had to bow your head when you said that word. "Make him well, Jesus." I said. I don't remember if I bargained or not. You know that we Catholics like to bargain with God. We like to get saints to intercede for us. We like to pull strings if we can. "Make him well, Jesus." I said again.

That night while the hospital was preparing the iron lung for Tommy, his fever broke. Tommy would live. His chest would balloon and swell forcing him to wear a brace lest his stomach would tumble out. His legs would be useless. He would not be able to take a deep breath, not cough deeply; none of it, not for the rest of his life. Tommy was sent to a special polio hospital in Galveston for four months.

When he got back home, everything was changed. Momma began to be less protective of her other children. She was now wholly committed to being Tommy's primary care provider. This meant that the rest of us were much freer than we had been before Tommy's polio. Momma wasn't such a nag to us anymore. The family stopped going to Boulder during the summers because it was too mountainous for Tommy in his wheelchair. Instead, we went to a different summer vacation house owned by Ma-Mee and Pa-Pa north of Beaumont near Woodville, Texas.

Momma let Tommy have his pet lamb come into the house. The lamb would stay in a box next to Tommy's bed and Tommy would feed the lamb with milk from a baby bottle. Often the lamb would get loose and we would chase it around. Tommy truly loved all living animate things, human or animal. He was a very good person to have around because he was so understanding. Overall, Tommy was very brave. How he could remain so pristine, so unmoved by the sadness of his situation is beyond me.

Maybe one reason is that our entire community loved and supported Tommy. Tommy's football friends at St. Anthony High School would carry him up and down the stairs in his wheel chair. Sometimes it was a three-story climb.

It was in those days of Tommy's illness during the swampy
September summer that my childhood ended. To say I was naive
would be wrong but I definitely was young and innocent. In some
ways, America in 1950 was young and innocent too. We had forcibly
reverted back to an earlier time. Yet the changes brought about
by the War had laid seeds. In the 1950s, American Society would
press those seeds down. Something new was on the horizon, the
beginnings which would shake our world to the core.

Chapter 6

As children, Peggy and I used to smoke used cigarette butts behind the house in the bushes. Back then there were no filters on cigarettes. Peggy and I started to go to the movies when I was thirteen and she was eleven. During the summer, Beaumont's picture show was air conditioned so kids used to spend every summer afternoon in the theater. In the school year, the children would stay in the picture show all afternoon on Saturdays. Everyone stayed for two features and several comedies until the afternoon heat subsided.

Murphy would drop us off at the movies and I would go to the bathroom there and put on orange Tangee lipstick. I wanted to look glamorous at the movies. When Peggy and I walked into the theater, all of our friends spread out in front us in descending rows. Children our age and younger joked and climbed over seats, boys tried to hold girl's hands and girls looked bashful, batting their eyes demurely. We all acted just the way we had been taught. I don't believe much in genetic predispositions, everything is learned from one role in one life to the new role in the next.

My self-esteem was low then. I was very self-conscious about what boys thought of me. I was starting to like them but I felt ugly. I had sucked my thumb until I was eight — which at the time, was just five years earlier — and from sucking my thumb, my teeth were parted in front. I wanted to get braces. I wanted to be beautiful. The Tangee lipstick was a safe accoutrement and helped me hide my teeth. Peggy and I would enter the theater and go our separate ways, she by her younger friends and me by mine.

One Saturday, I met a cute boy who was two years older than me who amazingly, wanted to spend time talking with me and getting to know me. I was very flattered and tried to not smile too much lest he see the gap between my teeth. We talked and talked and I hardly watched the films.

After the day was over, all the children shuffled out of the movies. On the way out to Murphy and our waiting car, I wiped my mouth clean of the lipstick with my petticoat. I couldn't let anyone see that I was trying to look more mature. I was emulating the older girls in town who I had seen wearing lipstick. I so wanted to be older when I was younger. It was that time in everyone's life when we can't wait to grow up.

Murphy brought Peggy and me home and Daddy was waiting for both of us when we came into the house. "Ruby!" he called to me from the sun porch. I walked over to the sun porch. Daddy told me to come in and close the doors. When I was seated in front of him he said sternly, "Ruby, did anything happen at the movies today?"

I swallowed hard. How could I tell Daddy what had happened? That I had worn lipstick and talked all afternoon long to a cute boy? How could he have known? I was sure I was in a lot of trouble. "No. No, Daddy. Nothing happened."

"Hmmmm," he said looking down. I held my breath. "Okay. You can go. Just be sure to tell me if anything happens in the future, okay?"

"Yes sir, Daddy." I said and rushed out of the sun porch.

I later found out that while we were at the movies, Peggy had been caught smoking by an usher. The usher had called the picture house's owner, Julius Gordon, to find out what to do. It just so happened that Julius Gordon was one of Daddy's friends from the local Rotary Club. Daddy was President of the Club and Mr. Gordon and Daddy had just come back to Mr. Gordon's office from a Rotary Luncheon.

"A little girl was caught smoking in the movies?" Mr. Gordon had said into the telephone receiver. Daddy's ears perked up. Daddy asked, "What's her name?" Mr. Gordon repeated Daddy's question into the telephone and upon hearing the answer hung up the phone without saying anything. Then he had looked at Daddy and said, "The little girl was Peggy Reed."

Peggy had been smoking not just in the bushes with me but also at the picture show.

Daddy didn't spank Peggy or anything. They stayed out on the sun porch for a while and Daddy just talked with Peggy. I think she learned her lesson because she never snuck around again. Daddy had a way of just talking to you to make you believe what he told you was right.

*

One day in 1984, during the midst of my rehabilitation, Ranny and I went to see a hospice patient. Since hospice work was the job I was planning on doing before the shooting, we felt it was time for me to get back to work. But now everything had changed. My perspective was totally different.

We went to see a young man whose name and face I can't remember. Ranny stayed out in the car and I went inside to the man's apartment. The man had cancer and was dying. I didn't talk at all. (In fact, you're not supposed to talk to the patients in hospice, you're supposed to listen).

As I sat in the man's room listening to him, I didn't feel like I belonged there. I was scared like he was. I figured I wouldn't be any help to him. I would need to get a ride to his apartment to see him again and I couldn't do much for him when I was at his apartment. Afterward, in the parking lot, I told Ranny that I didn't want to see anymore patients like that man again.

It took me a few years to understand why I didn't want to work with hospice patients. The truth is that I had come too close to death myself. I didn't want to see death up that close anymore. I had spent months in hospitals. It was too easy to relate with the hospice patients and I wanted to get away from them. I wanted to be distracted from death.

I believe our ultimate subconscious fear is death. This fear of death is the thing which creates all of our other fears. Out of this fear, we have created some sort of "divine" spiritual security. We want to believe in a life everlasting. We want to guard against death. We want life to continue, no matter how miserable it might be. All of this is a game. None of it is true.

"Now" is truth. That we will die is true. It is possible that we don't have souls; that souls are an invention just to make ourselves feel safe and secure in the face of death.

I feel that if a person faces existence now and also faces the reality of death, then he or she is on a path toward his or her enlightenment.

Personally, I believe that we all have souls. And when combined, we have the universal soul. But I can't convince anyone of this. Each of you has to experience enlightenment for yourself.

As I moved into my teen years, I became popular at St. Anne's Elementary School and at St. Anthony's High School. In the sixth grade, I was elected to be a cheerleader. Since I had "bird legs," (Tommy's nickname for me) I wanted to be sexy and curvy. So I got a hold of Momma's dress shoulder pads and with the pads I layered my hips to give myself a looking-glass curve. The boys didn't know what hit them. I really was the "cat's meow."

A year later, I decided I needed braces to fix the gap in my teeth that had developed from my thumb sucking. Momma said I didn't need them but I insisted on it. So the summer before high school, I marched over to the orthodontist's office (which was 1 block from my family's home) and pronounced that I needed braces. Momma paid for it.

Though I was only supposed to wear one rubber band on each side of my teeth to correct my overbite I put four mini-rubber bands on each side. The orthodontist was amazed at how quickly my teeth and overbite corrected. I smile to myself now, thinking of his expression. I was always in a hurry. After six months, the braces came off. At 15, with my braces off and my developing body, the boys were looking. I wanted them to look.

To the world, I had only one personality. "External Ruby" excelled at school, did cheerleading, sang in the choir, joined the Pep Squad, the Latin Club, CYO, Typing club, Sodality and Altar Club ... I was confident, smart, lovable, pious and many boys liked me. But internally, I was very insecure. I didn't know all of what lay inside of me and what did manifest during my adolescence was a great need for security. I was my Momma's girl (unbeknownst to me) and though I wanted more than anything to not be like Momma, I had been raised by a mourning mother — so that I would constantly strive for gratification from others. While trying to love other people, I didn't feel that I deserved that same love in return.

I was excited about high school. I didn't know what would happen but St. Anthony's High School lived up to all my expectations.

My four best friends and I planned how we'd get to school the first day, what we would wear and who we would sit by. My four best friends were Anne, Arlene, Arvilla, and Lynn. We were inseparable. I joined every club I could with the intent that in my Senior Yearbook, it would show all of the organizations I had been a part of, thus proving how popular I had been. Unfortunately, when my Senior Year finally came around the editors of the yearbook didn't list the organizations each senior had been involved with. Instead, the Senior class voted as a whole on each class member's attributes. I was: Frolicsome, Adventuresome, and Gay.

Anyway, I really loved high school. Changing classes was a real treat because all through elementary school we had only been in one classroom with the same teacher for the entire day. Now we had seven different teachers over one day's time. The classes were more specialized and we actually had to walk from classroom to classroom.

All of our teachers were nuns, of course. At St. Anne's Elementary school, we had a Belgium sect of nuns teaching us, named the sisters of St. Mary of Namure. As a girl, I had thought that all of these teacher/nuns were flat-chested with pockets which went down to their ankles. Even as a teenager at St. Anthony's High School, we still only had nuns, this time Dominican Nuns. Mass continued to be held before classes every morning.

In high school, I began having crushes on boys. The first crush I had was on Willy Novak. He was a Senior when I was a Freshman. At a CYO (Catholic Youth Organization) meeting, he asked me to dance. I lived off that experience for a year. I'd get my four friends to tell me what he said, how he looked. They'd go through it and through it with me, and then I would do the same thing for them and the boys they liked.

Ponytails had come into popularity in the 1950s and I liked the look; however, I felt my ears stuck out too much on the sides. One night, I decided to scotch tape down my ears before I went to bed hoping that they would be flat when I woke up in the morning. When I woke up, did my ears hurt! I tried taking the tape off them, which was excruciating. Eventually I got off the tape but I found out that my ears were beet red. That morning I went to mass with my scarf wrapped around my head. I never took it off the entire day. As you can see, I was very self-conscious when I was a teenager.

Our adolescence follows us. Though we may be thirty-five or fifty-five, parts of those bridge years from childhood to adulthood still affect us. I was self-conscious all my life. It has only been in the last fifteen years or so that I have decided to say "the hell with it." I'm going to live hourly.

*

As my rehabilitation continued, I felt I was useless and I wanted to feel useful. I would have worked as a janitor, I wouldn't have cared. I wanted to be good for something in my world. Since I was from a puritanical, pragmatic society, I felt if I couldn't work then I was useless. Time went by and all the work I was doing — all the rehabilitation — was ultimately to make myself useful again, not a burden to everyone. As you know, I couldn't do anything for myself. I couldn't even go anywhere in town by myself.

Alone, I could only go to places that were close to my house. For example, in the summer of 1984, I pushed my wheelchair blocks and blocks to Audubon Park. This was a big accomplishment for me. However, beyond walking a few blocks around my house, I couldn't do much else.

I felt very alone. Ranny and Mary Jane and the rest of my family and friends were helpful and loving but I didn't feel like anyone ever connected with "me."

I realize now that no one can connect with anyone. In fact, we are all alienated in a way. Fighting against this alienation is the mind's ego dreaming of an escape. But there is no escape. We can only be friends with our alienation. We can only understand it. We can only get closer to it. This is a very difficult process. It takes several lifetimes.

*

My early forays back out into the community were with family members. Either my brother Ranny, my sister, Peggy, or one of my children would take me in my wheelchair somewhere.

I remember I used to dream of working at Woolworths as a cashier. As I went out more and more, I decided that I needed to find a volunteer job. I wanted to prove to myself that I was a capable person. I had to prove to myself that I could do something.

*

When I became a Sophomore, it was understood that I would start dating. Years earlier, my sister, Mary had started dating as a Sophomore and I got the same privileges. The boy who I most wanted to date was Tommy. Most of the men that I have liked in my life have been older than me, but Tommy was my age. He came from a broken family. His father had died and then his mother remarried. The new marriage hadn't worked out and they got divorced. Divorcing was very rare in the 1950s.

Tommy drove a convertible with the top down and he would drink beer after school. It was known that he was wild and many of the girls were interested in him. Why do we women want the wild child, the bad boy? When we are young, that passionate boy who is rebelling against the staid life of our families is used as our symbol. In the 1950s, women were much less free than men and so maybe by idolizing boys like Tommy, we were acting out our own rebelliousness.

Actually all youngsters are rebelling. When adolescents become fully conscious of life, they realize the traps and the control that society has had over them from childhood. In this way, teenage rebellion is natural and important to a healthy society. I believe that rebelliousness ultimately stems from an internal quest for the revolution of freedom and complete personal awareness. One must always be awake no matter the age. For people to regress, be they 17 or 87, is for them to fall back into fear and ego.

Unfortunately, kids get trapped in their adolescent understanding of rebellion. For many of them, alcohol or drugs are the key to opening the mind, the key to some fictitious "truth." The reality, however, is that all truth is within us right now. Everything is okay. At this moment — even if everything is confused and problematic — it is still okay. Nothing is necessary, the world is open and the canvas is always white.

This makes me think I should publish a book and just have all the pages be blank white pages. It shouldn't be a diary, just a book of white pages.

*

Tommy used to speed past my house trying to impress me. I really did like him. We couldn't have company in the evening so Tommy came to my house a few times in the afternoon. When Tommy met Tilly (who we all called "Vi" for Viola up until then) he said, "Why you look just like a Tilly!" and everyone laughed! From then on everyone, called Vi, "Tilly," and that is the name I've used for her in this book.

Everyone liked Tommy in my family. He was very funny and very sweet. He was mysterious, too, and interesting. I imaged that Tommy was like James Dean. James Dean was everything to us girls back in the 50s. He was enigmatic and handsome. We all thought James Dean was the "cat's meow," and secretly, we all thought he was sexy, but no one ever came out and said the word "sexy."

Tommy came over to the house a lot and spent time with me and I think he wanted to ask me out but he never did. Eventually, Daddy took me aside and told me that Tommy was always welcome to come over and spend time with the family but that I was not to date him. Daddy said he had heard some bad things about Tommy, that Tommy was drinking and partying and that Tommy wouldn't be a good match for me.

I obeyed Daddy and let Tommy understand that I just wanted to be his friend.

*

My Junior year was wonderful. I was a cheerleader and I was elected the female favorite from our class (it must have been my padded hips). I had a crush on Dewy Doga who was a year older than I. He had eyes that changed colors with the seasons. He had some Choctaw Indian in him. I danced with him several times at CYO meetings before I got the nerve to ask him out. It was Twirp Week, when all the girls asked the boys out, so I asked him to a dance. We had a wonderful time.

After the dance, we went to the local teenage hangout called "The Pig Stand." Opal was our waitress. She walked out of the diner to Dewy's car and took our order. She brought our food to us and hung a tray on the side of Dewy's car. After eating some fries and a hamburger, we drove to the local Baptist Church's large parking lot. That was the meeting point.

It was about ten o'clock at night and the parking lot was empty. All of us Catholic kids formed a circle with our cars. We all turned on our radios to the same station and proceeded to dance. It was 1956. Elvis poured out of our cars.

This was called "street dancing." The boys danced with the girls, each couple together, outside of their cars. People were burning things at Elvis concerts, judges everywhere were pronouncing that he should never twist or gyrate or imitate sex at a show. They would point at Elvis with their shaking anvils and decry how he was deteriorating the youth of America.

Elvis would just sit there, smiling. At that moment, young Elvis was perfect. The purveyors of "morality" or "honorability" were telling Elvis we couldn't dance, couldn't sing black music, couldn't be free and young. It didn't matter. After Elvis' appearance on the Steve Allen Show (where Steve Allen forced Elvis to sing "Hound Dog" to a basset hound) Elvis told his audience that, "You know, those people in New York are not going to change me none. I'm going to show you what the real Elvis is like tonight." He was unstoppable.

All through the South, all through the North, adolescents crowded to his shows. We heard he had collapsed on stage after one musical set, his doctor telling this young ex-truck driver from Memphis, "to take it easy, you do more in a span of twenty minutes than an average laborer does in eight hours."

It wasn't just that he was sexy on stage. Elvis was blowing the lid off of every piece of carefully orchestrated American morality. Our generation was — for split seconds — free. We were young and innocent and like Elvis we just loved the music, we didn't care that it had been Black people's music. Back then, with society as it was, only a Southern White boy could have taken all of the underground Black music and given it to the world.

The adults didn't know what to do. Once Momma had caught Peggy and me dancing in our room to a rock-n-roll record called "It's not the meat. It's the motion." Upon seeing the record, Momma had promptly smashed the little 45 rpm disc into little pieces. Her tight, tight curls had seemed so inconsequential and unfortunate that night. She had stood in front of us, her eyebrows glowering and brutal and her face very, very old.

*

As a little girl, I remember Murphy listening to the local Black station, KJET. At night, Murphy would go out to the Black bars dressed like a hipster. Back then, the black music wasn't a problem because it stayed with the Black people. But now ten years later, thanks to Elvis Presley, white kids were listening to it and Mommas and Daddies all over America were loosing control of their children.

For all these reasons they sent Elvis off to the army. He was never the same when he came back from Germany. They made Elvis into Frank Sinatra. He had grown up.

That night in 1956, Dewy Doga danced with me. Black music played on. Under the Beaumont stars I was happy. I was safe. I really loved Dewy. I closed my eyes and felt utterly protected. I felt that here was a person I could be with outside of home. I wouldn't be afraid of the world as long as Dewy loved me back.

Later, on the drive to my house I told Dewy how special he was to me. I told him how much I cared for him. I didn't use the word "love"; I just told him I really liked him. He parked on the street in front of my house and fell silent, staring at his steering wheel. Dewy didn't say anything for a while. Then finally, "I like you too, Ruby. I'm going away to college next year. And, and ... I don't want to be tied down." I nodded. It was okay. I was in shock. Tears were in the back of my eyes, and down my throat, but I wouldn't let him see them. I hugged him goodbye and I walked up alone to the door of the house.

My best friends Anne, Arlene, Arvilla, and Lynn were at home, waiting for me in the upstairs hall. I walked in and closed the door and started to sob. They rushed over to me. To this day, I believe in being honest. It may hurt at first, but I've always been glad Dewey was.

*

My first volunteer job after the shooting was at a gift card shop. The owner of the gift card shop was a girl who had babysat for Pio and me years earlier. She was running the gift store at One Shell Square in New Orleans' Business District on the basement floor. This job was ideal for me because it allowed me to practice my numbers. I wanted to find a volunteer job which would help me count.

The card shop was housed in one room and there were greeting cards everywhere. There were knickknacks on the walls and a raised desk with a cash register on it. I didn't get that much practice with numbers because the register automatically told me how much change to give a customer. Still though, I was learning and I was out of the house. Back then, I guess I looked a bit odd with the patch over my eye pounding away at the cash register. But it didn't matter to me. I was getting back in the world.

*

My Senior year in high school was a let-down. For one thing, there were no older boys. Another thing was that I had to decide if I wanted to go to college or to the convent. Three of my four best friends, Anne, Arlene, and Arvilla had decided on the convent. I was really conflicted about this. On the one hand, there was the convent and the belief that I was doing God's will. On the other hand, there was the challenge that I had never met. I had never gone away from home. I had always been protected. A piece of me knew I had to face it: I had to experience being alone, not depending on anyone but myself. So the choice was really very clear and yet I still agonized over it.

I used to throw up every night for six weeks trying to decide what to do. For the first week, poor Tilly helped me clean up the floor by my bed until she insisted that I keep a bucket next to the bed at all times until I had decided what I was going to do with my life.

I decided the hardest thing to do and the biggest challenge was to go off to college. The real problem wasn't college or the convent, the real problem was me leaving home. I felt that if I wanted to go into the convent after college I could, but I had to really test myself and be alone.

To this end, the summer before I left Beaumont for New Orleans and Loyola University, I went to my friend Dallas Hill's rented beach house. She and I and her family stayed on the Gulf of Mexico together. This was my first test away from home. I felt good. I was ready to go to New Orleans.

Chapter 7

It had been a long ride, about six hours. On the ride through Southern Louisiana, I had thought back to visiting New Orleans as a child and playing with my siblings in the French Quarter. I had heard that New Orleans was very old (by our puny American standards) and exciting. Everyone knew that the politics were dirty and that the music tradition was rich.

Now I was here and my heart was pumping. I could hardly speak. I kept looking at the many unfamiliar homes along the streets of New Orleans. Here I was just a speck of dirt, petrified of all these new people. I could hardly press the gas peddle. I inched around the city until I finally came to my new dormitory — Immaculata.

The Immaculata dorm was run by an order of nuns from Spain called the Daughters of Jesus. These same Daughters came over from Spain not knowing a word of English. When they got off the boat in America they walked from the Nashville Street Port Landing in New Orleans along the Mississippi River to Loyola University. Somehow they got word that there was a house for sale along St. Charles Avenue three blocks away from Loyola. They made a deal with the university that in exchange for opening a girl's dormitory, the nuns would be able to take courses at Loyola for free. When I met them, only a few of the nuns spoke English, most of them still only spoke Spanish.

I sat out in my convertible, looking up at the dormitory. I was so alone. My heart was beating very fast. I went up to the front door and rang the doorbell. A nun answered it. I felt a rush of relief. At the time, I believed that nuns and priests could do no wrong so it was very reassuring to go into a world I knew.

I couldn't tell the nun's age. I never can actually. They always have the most beautiful complexions. Back before Vatican II, all of the nuns appeared in public in full regalia and this nun was no different. In their cloistered areas, no one knew whether or not the nuns were more relaxed. My sister Peggy was a nun for four years but I never asked her how the nuns were together when they were away from the public eye.

The nun let me in and humbly showed me the dormitory with her hands either in her pockets or wrapped under her scapular. She believed she was just a servant of God.

In hindsight, it was sad. The only choices a Catholic woman felt she had was being a school teacher, a nun, or getting married. That poor nun didn't seem to realize that she wasn't a servant of God but instead that she was the Goddess herself! Oh well, I digress.

The Daughters of Jesus did everything with austerity and conservation in mind. Nothing was wasted. Everything was given up to the Lord. For example, when the nuns would kneel down at the pews during mass their habits were pulled up a bit and their feet were exposed. One could see that they wore sandals made of old tire rubber. Also the Daughters of Jesus cut paper napkins in half to conserve the amount of napkin we would use at the table.

I have always agreed with this bedrock of frugal living. I hate spending money recklessly. In this, I am still very Catholic even though I have thrown off much of my Catholicism. You can always take some truth from even a sleeping institution or person; nothing and no one is inherently bad.

My new bedroom was on the second floor of the dormitory. It was very large but it wasn't big enough to house five girls. A year later — as a Sophomore — I petitioned the head proprietress of Immaculata — Mother Ima — to remove one of the girls and let only four girls stay in the room. It didn't make things that much better but it helped. Soon after seeing my new room, I met my new roommates. Everyone seemed very nice. In a few minutes, I went down to my car and with the help of some of the other girls, I unloaded the car, bringing all of my things up to the room.

Being here in New Orleans didn't seem so bad. It was going to be a snap! I really wasn't nervous at all and the fear I had felt upon coming to New Orleans was gone. All of the Freshmen at Loyola University came a week early. It was Orientation Week. That first week felt like it was only a vacation away from my family and friends in Beaumont. In that first week, I learned about our campus and the city. All over Loyola University, there were ex-military Quonset Huts. The university used them for makeshift classrooms and mess halls.

We also had to register for classes. All of the Freshmen at Loyola had to go to Dr. Horne's orientation. He asked us what we were going to major in. Everyone was paging through the school syllabus trying to figure out what they were going to study. I raised my hand tentatively.

*

When I had been in Eighth Grade at St. Anne's Elementary School, Father Swilley had taught us about St. Thomas Aquinas' Five Proofs for the existence of God. From this beginning, I had needed Philosophy in my life. I still need it today.

Anne's death and Tommy's polio were always with me; these questions were like a scent which was behind everything. Even as a child, I had always asked myself why Anne had died and why Tommy got ill. Through St. Aquinas' syllogisms, I was able to believe in God. I still didn't feel I had the answers to my questions about Tommy and Anne but at least, I believed in a God that someday could give me the answer to these impossible questions.

So I was convinced I wanted to learn Philosophy. When I raised my hand, Dr. Horne looked down at me and said, "Yes, my dear. You have a question about the School of Education?"

"Sir," I spoke like a mouse in a large room of blunt metal traps, "Where is the Philosophy section in the syllabus?" He was almost at a loss for words. "Philosophy? Why do you want that?" "It's what I want to study."

"Girls always do education or nursing. Why don't you do that and make it easier on yourself? No woman wants to understand such a boring topic as Philosophy." I said nothing. I just watched him. After a bit of time, he sighed, somewhat reserved, and showed me how to sign up for Philosophy courses. The week of orientation went by easily. I was beginning to get used to this vacation. It was easy being away from home.

The girls in my room were nice. We all became friends. In the mornings, they and I shared a communal bathroom with two other rooms of girls. In all, it was fifteen of us trying to get into the bathroom in the morning. The nuns gave us half a towel rack for our towels and a third of a shelf for our toiletries. I liked to call the bathroom the "Boston Club" after a very exclusive New Orleans club because getting into it was very difficult.

On the first Monday of the second week at Loyola University, classes began. I didn't know anything about hours or how college classes worked. Being a very little fish in a big pond was not much fun, especially the first day. I went to my first class. People were everywhere. They lined the halls and the corridors. There was no air conditioning at all. The lecture hall was hot and humid. Everyone was sweating. The desks were piled into the room.

I realized I was all alone now at the university. I was all alone in this big city. My heart began to pound. Suddenly, I wanted to go back home … home to Beaumont and Momma and Daddy and the old friends and the street dancing at night. I wanted to be far away from this vast place where I was just like everyone else and yet I didn't fit in! How could I fit in? Everyone here was different and individual and doing whatever they pleased. This wasn't the regimented life I had known for eighteen years with Momma and Daddy. And though Loyola was a Catholic school run by Jesuit priests, here everyone was free. You could do what you wanted.

I edged into the lecture hall. I could hardly breathe. This was not a vacation, this was my new life! I was petrified! How could I live

here! In terror, I sat down. I could not speak. I would not speak.
I would be fine. I would pretend as if all of this wasn't really
happening, and that I was just in a momentary panic and it would
all pass. But half-way through the hour of my first university class,
I had said three entire rosaries in my mind. I don't even remember
what the professor said that first day.

By that night, my fear had grown. Everything was worse at night.
I was sure The Boogey Man was back under my bed. My lack of
home and my need for it was very strong.

Tuesday was worse. I cried myself to sleep. Wednesday, I was
crying in the morning when I woke up. Everyone heard me crying
in our dorm room. Some of my roommates tried to console me but
I wouldn't listen. I went to classes that day anyhow even though
I was a wet, weeping mess. I didn't care that everyone on campus
saw the tears on my face. It was no secret how scared I was.

On Wednesday, I didn't know what to do so I went to the Dean of
the University. He was a middle-aged stern looking Jesuit who had
no idea how to deal with a weepy young girl. I looked at him for
help and he just swallowed hard. I cried louder and harder. I had
heard that the Jesuits wore "hair shirts" which were woolen prickly
shirts so as to offer up suffering to God every day of their lives. This
Jesuit's shirt must have been on extra tight that day because he
didn't even change his stern expression when I cried. He shuffled
some papers on his desk and looked furtively at me. "Um, well, why
don't you go see Miss Parrino, the Dean of Women?"

Miss Rosie Parrino was Loyola University's first Dean of Women.
She would become a bit of a legend on campus in her time but in
1957 she was just starting out in her position. In fact, this was her

first year. She was about five years older than me, slightly plump
with warm eyes. I felt like I could be open to her.

After I explained my dilemma, she smiled as if she had heard this
all before (and of course, she had heard it all before), "Well, now,
Ruby, what I want you to do is go back to the dormitory and get
some good rest. I want you to hold out for just two more days. On
Friday afternoon, after classes you can go back to Beaumont, Texas,
and see how you feel. We'll take things from there once you are in
Beaumont. Can you do that for me?"

"Yes, ma'am, I guess ... I guess I could." I said.

*

It was hard for me to take taxis after the shooting because I couldn't
count and making change was very difficult.

Once I started a job, I was worried that I would have to take taxis
everywhere but New Orleans had a special service for handicapped
people called "Handicab" that would take handicapped people
wherever they wanted to go in the city. "Handicab" is still in
existence to this day.

Handicab, however, took quite a while to get around because the
Handicab was very full. Still I got to work on time. Coming home,
however, was another matter. I had to wait sometimes an hour
and a half standing on the sidewalk in the business district of New
Orleans. I was alone with all the regular people filing past me.

"Dammit, I needed a car!" I thought. I needed to be a whole human
being again! Just about at that time, I got my driver's license
renewed. I probably should never have driven given my physical

limitations but at least driving gave me the freedom that I needed in my life.

After about a year of working at the gift card shop, the owner told me she was moving to St. Louis and closing the shop. I had to find a new volunteer job. By then, I could easily go to new volunteer jobs. Eventually, I ended up getting two jobs, one at Children's Hospital near my house and the other as an assistant librarian which I had for about two years. We used the Dewy Decimal system. I worked Tuesday and Thursday afternoons organizing the books. The job at Children's Hospital lasted over ten years. I packaged the mailing envelopes for the hospital.

I used to meet for lunch once a week with a group of fellow workers. We were all very close and talked about our problems. In many ways, it was like a group therapy session.

I was so glad to be of some use to the world. It is natural and normal for the ego to feel pleasure when it is useful. However, the desire to be useful is an unhealthy priority. One always has to be cognizant of one's desires.

I arrived back in Beaumont Friday night. I remember that it was really quiet, much different than Loyola and New Orleans. When I got home, I was so excited to see Momma, Daddy, Tilly, Peggy and Tommy. I drove through town seeing all the old sights that I had just left a week and a half earlier. It was all very familiar and safe. I was happy. Momma and Daddy and Tilly greeted me with odd looks on their faces. "Hi, Ruby," they said tentatively.

"Hey!" I hugged them all very tightly. They didn't hug me back so firmly.

When I came into the house Peggy was sitting on the couch. She was a Junior in high school and in two years time she would be in the convent. She was nice but she didn't understand why I was home. "I just missed y'all so much!" I said hugging Peggy. Peggy gave me the same sort of odd look Momma, Daddy, and Tilly had given me.

Tommy was in the back yard when I came home. He was sitting in his wheel chair feeding the dogs and his pet goat (which had gotten quite big by then). Tommy was studying at Lamar; a university in Beaumont. He would study there and at Texas A&I. He tried several different jobs around Beaumont and eventually settled at a bank. He hugged me when I came over to him but he also didn't seem to understand why I was back so soon.

Mary was married by this time. She had children and a husband and I didn't even see her that entire weekend I was in Beaumont. Ranny, the special one, wasn't in Beaumont either. After finishing high school in 1950, he had gone to college at Catholic University in Washington D.C. and from college, had gone right into the military for two years. By the time he got out of the service, it was 1956. Ranny had been lucky enough to be stationed in Italy when he was a soldier and had learned fluent Italian. He also had traveled to many places in Europe.

When he came back to Beaumont, he didn't seem to know what to do with himself there. He around the countryside with his new artist and theater friends. I suspect he knew that Beaumont was too small for him but he wasn't sure yet where he fit in, and if he did.

He had studied Architecture and Political Science in college and could have done a lot with those degrees but nothing seemed to stick with Ranny. He just drifted.

Then in the summer of 1957, only a few months before I went off to school at Loyola, Ranny went out one night drinking with some of his friends. The next morning Ranny had come home with tears in his eyes. We had all just returned from morning mass and were eating breakfast. Ranny entered the house crying. He announced to us with a quivering voice that he had seen the most beautiful thing ever. It was "all light, all colors," he said.

Momma immediately told him, "I'm gonna call Father Halub." Father Halub was our priest.

We later found out that Ranny had been out in the countryside drinking with some of his friends and had seen this bright light in front of him. The light had touched him; it was so beautiful and translucent.

For the rest of Ranny's life, he could never talk about that moment without crying. Not out of pain, but simply because it was so beautiful. This was his awakening experience. Had he seen a UFO? Was he on drugs? We still don't know. Ranny did eventually go and speak with Father Halub. After months of talking about his experience, Father Halub had impressed upon Ranny that he, Randolph Compton Reed Jr., had been given a special charge. Father Halub believed that Ranny was called by God to be a chaste servant. Ranny was to become a monk.

I'm not sure if Ranny was actively homosexual at that time. (The story goes that when Daddy found out Ranny was gay, Daddy slapped him across the face). Ranny was twenty-six years old hanging around with artistic friends so it is a good bet that he was already gay. At any rate, Ranny, decided to become a monk. In order to become a monk, Ranny had to give away all of his earthly possessions. He gave all of his inherited money and clothing to his friends and family. In doing this, Ranny divested himself of all his worldly goods which was quite a lot of worldly goods that he had inherited. But now he was free of his old life and ready to approach God.

The order Ranny chose to enter was the Carthusian monks, a French-based order, one of the oldest monastic orders in the Roman Catholic Church. Though Ranny had learned French and Latin in high school, he went to a Carthusian retreat in Vermont to learn fluent French and Latin. He left for Vermont in 1959. When I returned back to Beaumont from Loyola University in September 1959, Ranny had already left home.

As ever, Ranny was a good student. He learned French and Latin quickly and was soon sent to the Chartreuse Mountains in France where the monks had their monastery since 1086. Upon arriving at the monastery, Ranny was put in a cell with thick walls and only fed through a slot in the door. He was just served bread and water every other day. If he wanted, the water could be substituted for wine. The monks prayed together seven times a day, even at night. This meant that they went from their cells once every three hours (no matter the time of day or night) to the Chapel and prayed. The only other time they left their cells was to eat dinner together. Besides an hour of recreation, it was a very solitary existence.

We teased Ranny that he must have at least liked the wine because he was in France and the Fathers of the Carthusian order had been making and selling their famous Chartreuse liqueur for hundreds of years.

Ranny wasn't able to deal with the hard lifestyle and after six weeks, he was back on a boat to the States. I don't know what to say about Ranny's inability to be a monk. It wasn't as if he did not have a very personal, very spiritual side. Ranny was beyond religion or dogma and this is probably why he couldn't connect with the clergy. Maybe, he just got homesick like I did and couldn't get over it.

He returned to Beaumont and proceeded to beg for his old things back! Well, I'm exaggerating. Most people were happy to give Ranny back his money and possessions. It was kinda funny. After getting his money back, Ranny bought a house in the countryside near Beaumont. He lived at that house for the rest of his life. Ranny had parties there and became something like a free-thinking village monk. His indoor bathroom was broken and he never bothered to fix it (though he had the money to do so). He would pee and defecate in his garden, which he called his Zen garden of weeds and wildflowers. And sometimes a lover might stay with him.

Ranny also liked the Caribbean; especially the Florida Keys. He bought a boat there in which he often stayed. At the end of his life, Ranny only owned five white Guayabera shirts, a few Bermuda shorts, a few long-sleeve shirts and a pair of blue jeans for winter. It was a comfortable life but later on, he told me he wished he had done more. I think Ranny always felt he was a failure. Ranny had a good degree from a good school. I had suggested to him that he ought to try to tutor kids going to college. He said that he felt it was too late to do that. He could have tutored people in Latin,

French, or Italian. It wasn't too late. He only believed in his mind it was too late.

I remember that Ranny's awakening experience and his time as a monk coincided with Pa-Pa Phelan's death. When Pa-Pa died, he was one of the most celebrated men of Texas. They buried him with all his Catholic regalia, title upon title lay on his chest. He wore the cloaks and badges of many a knightly Catholic order. Pa-Pa was a great man. After the funeral, Ma-Mee announced that she and Pa-Pa had decided that upon one of their deaths, their home would be donated to the Church and that the church would convert their mansion into a hospital. And that is just what happened. Pa-Pa and Ma-Mee's home became St. Elizabeth's Hospital in Beaumont.

*

Years later after Pa-Pa died, Pio and I and our little children would come from New Orleans to bury Ma-Mee. With the rest of the Phelans and Reeds, we laid Ma-Mee to rest in the cemetery next to Pa-Pa. That was in the 1960s when the old was giving way to something totally new. Now the new is old and just giving way. Life is funny like that, we transition and you don't realize it when you are young but the next generation is everything.

Ma-Mee was buried with all the titles and regalia beholden to a wife of one of the country's most important Catholic men. Years later, freer and more awake, I wondered and still wonder to this day about that matriarch. Who was she? Was she just Ma-Mee? Who was this Johanna Cunningham Phelan? Maybe Hanna to her friends and peers? Why do women always outlive their men? Why do matriarchs continue on when patriarchs die off?

*

After seeing my family for a few hours, I went out and drove around Beaumont. I wanted to call my friends and go dancing and have fun! But no one was around. Three of them had gone off to be nuns and the fourth was in college. I drove out to Pa-Pa Phelan's old home. The church had taken the mansion over by then and was busy converting it to the Catholic hospital, St. Elizabeth's. I looked out over Pa-Pa's lawn. It was dark and damp on that wet September night. I remembered playing with other children on that grass almost twenty years earlier.

It hit me: I didn't belong here in Beaumont. It was over and past for me. No one was around and my life here was over even if I didn't want it to be. The trees told me this, the sky shouted it. I looked into the sky. I was a lone star in the Lone Star State. Everything was very quiet. It was time to leave and I'd only been back home from New Orleans for three hours. But I knew Beaumont wasn't my home anymore.

I went back to Momma and Daddy's house. They were waiting up for me in the living room when I walked in, listening to the radio. Daddy turned it down as I entered. Both of them still had that strange look on their faces they had when I had arrived a few hours earlier. I understood it now. I felt a little shame. It was as if I had been wrong to have come back to Beaumont. I had picked freedom and education. Why was I allowing myself to be stunted? They were giving me permission to leave and do something else.

"Did you enjoy seeing Beaumont?" Daddy touched his chin with his forefinger.

I said that I did. Then I said, "I'll be going back to New Orleans after Mass on Sunday. I just wanted to say hello to y'all."

"That sounds nice, Ruby." Momma said smiling.

I went up to bed. I slept very comfortably. I couldn't wait to get back to New Orleans.

*

Twenty-five years after the shooting, I can do just about anything I want except run. I can walk almost anywhere. I can see. I can hear. I can speak about Philosophy and politics (Talking one to one is still easier for me).

I do still have limitations. The semi-paralysis doesn't allow me to move very quickly. I have to take my time.

Maybe this is one of the reasons I had my spiritual awakening. After the shooting, I had to take my time with everything. I used to be in such a hurry before the shooting. Imagine that, forty-four years of life and always in a hurry. I was fast to go into school, fast to go off to college, fast to get married, fast to have five children, and eventually fast to get divorced and find my own life.

I think the main thing I've learned over the years is patience. You can't hurry patience. It just comes gradually.

I walk every day now, usually about two miles. The walk is definitely very deliberate for me. I am very conscious about each crack in the sidewalk or on street black top. Sometimes I get really tired coming home and I think, "Ruby, just one step at a time." I'm able to see the movement of people and insects and flowers blooming and how the sunlight shines. I feel blessedness to my life, to life in general and I know each of us can experience this blessedness. But you may not find it the way I did. In the end, I worked very hard for my rehabilitation. And each day, I continue to work hard. But as I've improved it has become a joyous effort.

*

The fear was gone and school was wonderful when I returned from Beaumont! Loyola University and New Orleans filled my time. I didn't get involved in all those school organizations I had back in high school except for the Philosophy Club. I was the sole member for one year!

I was alive with learning. Books and their new ideas fascinated me. I had, up until then, not seen much of life. I was, and am until this day, innocent. I think innocence is a state of mind, a choice one makes. Of course, much happens to us dependent on our past lives and our progress toward the Goddess and God that we are, however much of this can be tied to choice ... that is, to a point. For instance, I had no choice whether or not to be shot. But I did have a choice whether I wanted to get fat and give up or stand up and fight. And I did have a choice that I wanted God to make my life difficult. Now I wanted to make me back like I was before.

*

It is like we have a blindfold put on us when we are conceived. We know who our parents are going to be and we know the big things that will happen in our lives. For whatever reason, it was my energy or karma or path to get shot. In retrospect, I can look at why it happened. Before I was shot, I was so comfortable where I was. But the shooting had to happen to me in order to wake up and become more conscious.

When I look back on how I was before the shooting and then after to the transformation in myself, I see that it was a road, a correct energy path that I had to follow. This transformation is what each cognizant being has to go through. We never meet anyone we don't know. Somewhere — at sometime — we meet. There are no accidents. It could have been pleasant or unpleasant but my karmic meeting happened and that is what I am face to face with everyday.

*

One thing about New Orleans that I wasn't prepared for was the amount of alcohol young people consumed. I mean some of them were allowed to drink when they were eleven or twelve years old, so they grew up consuming even more alcohol In college, I would go to a friend's house and his or her parents would just serve us alcohol automatically. Culturally, this was strange for me coming from Texas, but New Orleans and Southern Louisiana have always been different from the rest of America.

The French settled in southern Louisiana in the early 1700s. The Port of New Orleans was America's largest port and the culture of south Louisiana became a hybrid of Southern, African, French and Caribbean cultures. The food and the music and the literature mixed, and by the time I was in New Orleans, there were Irish in New Orleans with accents which sounded like they could have been from Dublin or Newark instead of the South. In the Ninth Ward, there were dark-skinned African—Americans from Mississippi who sounded like they were from Mississippi while in the Treme District, there were light-skinned Creole African—Americans whose parents still spoke Creole French as their native language.

During the 1950s, Louis Prima was a popular national singer who always proudly told his audience that he was, "An Italian—American from New Orleans!" In the late 1950s, there was a

young up-and-coming Chinese restaurateur in New Orleans
called Harry Lee who spoke English with the thickest cowboy
accent you could ever imagine. Harry Lee would eventually
come to dominate the political and law enforcement structure of
Jefferson Parish, an important neighboring area of Metropolitan
New Orleans. All this was — and is — New Orleans. We were, and
are, a massive mix of peoples put down together in one of the
world's most interesting ports.

Ultimately, New Orleans is a city of neighborhoods and
neighborhood loyalties. In 1957, all us different Americans lived
together in the same neighborhoods. We spent more time outdoors
because very few homes were air conditioned then. Sitting on your
stoop and having a conversation with any passerby was the norm.
New Orleans had more trees for shade and less pavement and so
there was less heat in the city.

In 2008, New Orleans, even after Hurricane Katrina, continues
to maintain the almost lost American traditions of communal
neighborhoods. America has become more individual and
consumeristic.

I feel that even the race situation in New Orleans — a topic which
is so discussed and so negatively portrayed in our national media,
is, in some ways, quite a bit better than in most American cities.
There are many neighborhoods in New Orleans that are alive with
what I call the "fudge-ripple effect," white and black people living
next door to one another.

Following my shooting, I have been so grateful for New Orleans.
There are few other major American cities where I can walk
from my house to a beauty parlor, a fine restaurant, a gas station,

a clothing store, and a major urban park and zoo. In most major cities, I would have to live in the suburbs and commute via car to a mall or a downtown area. Though I am handicapped, I am able to be more independent here than anywhere else. Plus, I have a lot of friends in New Orleans who are like family.

*

When I was in school at Loyola University, I spent most of my time Uptown where the college crowd was. New Orleans is split into many divisions but the most recognizable division is between Uptown and Downtown. Canal Street separates the city into two halves. The battle over which is the better side to live has raged between New Orleanians for hundreds of years. It won't be solved by my book — though, of course, it is plain that Uptown is the best place to live!

Most people believe Uptown is a bit higher class. Tulane University and Loyola University are Uptown. Also the mansions along St. Charles Avenue are Uptown. The Garden District and Audubon Park are all Uptown. We have restaurants Uptown like Commander's Palace, La Madeline and Camela Grill, and life is a bit more refined Uptown. The bars are nicer, the cars shinier, and the people are more respectful.

For me, Downtown is the bawdy drunken place. The French Quarter is Downtown. The dance clubs and strip bars are Downtown. All manner of drunken, drug-addled behavior is Downtown. The streets of the French Quarter often smell of urine and vomit. Please don't misunderstand, there are some wonderful things Downtown. The French Quarter is historically beautiful and besides that, there is Armstrong Park in the Treme district. Also the Ninth Ward and the old Faubourg Marigny districts have many traditional bars and restaurants. But as for myself, I've always lived Uptown and I like living Uptown.

I've never been a drinker. I didn't drink in college at all and it took until I was around thirty before I'd even have a Scotch Old-Fashioned with my best friend, Mary Jane, on Sunday evenings. I guess it was part of my innocence. Back in the 50s, almost everyone drank. It just had never been for me. I would go out with them and laugh and have fun and be able to get up and do things in the morning that they couldn't with their hangovers. I really wanted to be awake and learn as much as I could.

The girls in Immaculata used to go upstairs to the third floor recreation area. The nuns used the area for storage so we girls would sit out among the old chests and luggage and turn on disjointed lights and talk. Most of the girls drank beer and joked around. It really was a good time. No one really ever got too drunk. It was just a good time to be with the girls. We used to tell the nuns that we were using the cans of beer to roll our hair on They believed us because we actually did use empty beer cans to roll our hair. And of course, beer is good to give your hair body and fullness. In the 50s, we used to be able to buy beer shampoo!

*

In 1958, I got the chance to ride in a Mardi Gras parade and be in a Pat Boone movie. It all started because one of my friends from Immaculata named Linda Trusty had a sister named Shirley who was a dance and posture instructor in New Orleans. One day, Linda took me to meet her older sister. Shirley looked at me and told me I should model and that she could teach me. I agreed and after a few posture lessons, I really was pretty good.

Shirley told me about a small part in a movie called "Mardi Gras" starring Pat Boone. The film and the part were to be shot in the winter and they were looking for a young model to be on one of the Mardi Gras floats.

Well, I tried out for the part and I got it! I didn't have any lines but Pat Boone was supposed to be in love with me and I was supposed to be a maid from a Mardi Gras Krewe. I rode in a Mardi Gras parade and they filmed me on a float. I also was filmed at the famous St. Louis Cathedral in Jackson Square in the heart of New Orleans.

I made $25 per day, which was pretty good for 1958. We shot my section over five days so by the end of my shooting I was $125 richer. Again back in 1958, $125 was a lot of money.

Mardi Gras itself wasn't as interesting as I had heard. The parades were big and long but the floats were old and some of the carriages that the parading Krewes used to pull their floats were from the 19th century. Even to this day, there are carriages in the Mardi Gras parades which are one hundred fifty years old! Nowadays, the flame carriers, or the Flambeaus, don't do that much. (But back when I first started at the university, would they ever dance!) They were wonderful to watch. And everyone tipped them very well. Unfortunately, no one tips anymore.

I wasn't much impressed with the Mardi Gras floats. In Beaumont, we had floats in parades but our floats were more elaborate and prettier. We used chicken wire stuffed with crepe paper. In Mardi Gras, they had painted floats. I always felt that painting floats was too easy. It was much harder to make a float out of crepe paper.

Nowadays, the floats in Mardi Gras are better than they were but still I am partial to the floats of Beaumont and my youth.

One of the things I have never been able to get over about Mardi Gras has been the waste of beads. These beads are a symbol of New Orleans Mardi Gras parading culture. As the floats pass people throng forward against the police barricades and shout, "Throw me somethin', mister!" The float riders toss bunches of multicolored beads into the crowd and the people wrestle with each other to get the shiny plastic necklaces.

However, after the parade and excitement are over the gutters are clogged with unclaimed Mardi Gras beads. The people have had their fun and have taken home a few beads but most of the rest lay unused. The fun is in seeing how many each person can catch.

My children went to school at the local Montessori Elementary and after Mardi Gras every year we used to take the beads we had collected to the school. The Montessori Method emphasizes conservation of all things and so in New Orleans they had a method by which they would heat the beads and melt them down into key chains and trinkets. At least this way, not all the beads were wasted.

New Orleans cuisine centers around sea food. Yuck! I've never been very interested in food to start with and I have especially never liked sea food. In fact, as a child I got by on ketchup sandwiches for lunch. Since the shooting, my olfactory sense has been greatly diminished (That's what happens when you get shot in the nose) and my taste has been halved. There doesn't seem to be much of a point to eat expensive food anymore. I will admit though that I occasionally like a good steak. This must be my Texan upbringing.

In college, I went once on a fancy date to Galatoire's, a famous French Quarter restaurant, with a young law student named Mo. It was a Friday and since New Orleans is one of the most Catholic cities in America, the restaurants tended to respect the pre-Vatican II non-meat fast on Fridays. Mo, who was from New Orleans, loved sea food and thought Galatoire's would be the perfect date for us. When I saw the menu though, I didn't know what to do. Given the choice of vegetables and sea food, I picked vegetables and ordered a plate of sliced tomatoes. They obliged my parochial Texan ways. Mo laughed and laughed at me.

I enjoyed going on dates when I was in school. A usual date in New Orleans in the late 50s centered around going to the movies and then to a jazz bar in the French Quarter. All of us college students were so poor that we didn't have the money to eat out at a restaurant. The only problem with dates was that Immaculata had a curfew. On Sunday through Thursday nights, the nuns would lock the outside dorm doors at 10 p.m. On Friday nights, the curfew was 12 a.m. and on Saturdays the doors would be locked at 1 a.m.

Well, suffice it to say, I missed the curfew a lot on the weekends. When we started college, the girls at Immaculata would open a window and lower a bunk bed ladder down to any wayward soul coming home past curfew. The late girl's date would give the girl a boost up to the ladder whereupon she would be pulled, ladder and all, up into the room. Eventually the nuns caught on to what we were doing and put locks on the windows. The first time my roommates and I realized that we couldn't be pulled up to the bedroom, the girls came down to the gazebo and took the door off the hinges so that we could get into the building. Since pulling the front door off its hinges couldn't be done all the time, I became

resigned to sleeping at friends' houses or in the cars of my dates
(Again, don't get the wrong idea).

In the morning, I would wake up and join the Daughters of Jesus
and a few girls from our dormitory at mass. The head of the
Daughters of Jesus, Mother Irma, would tease me with that Spanish
accent of hers, "You, Ruby, must join the sisters! When will you
join, Ruby?" And I'd blush, "No, no ... not now."

Mary Jane was also a great force for my rehabilitation. She was so
wonderful and caring. Mary Jane was my closest support through
all of my trials. She strongly believed that I needed to get back to
being able to run in the morning and this became one of my major
goals after the shooting. I participated in the Crescent City Classic
in 1984. Mary Jane and other friends pushed me in my wheelchair
for the race's 6.2 miles. I also participated again in the Crescent
City Classic in 1985 and this time I was rehabilitated enough to
push my own wheelchair for the last half a mile.

Everyone cheered me on. I guess it made them feel good. I felt
good. I was happy. I cried out of joy that I got my wheel chair over
the line. Yet, as everyone came over to me, congratulating me, I
felt that they were almost trying to make themselves feel better.
They were trying to placate their own guilt at seeing me. I didn't
participate again in the Crescent City Classic until much later. And
by then, I was a totally different person. By then, I had come out of
my cocoon. I had awakened.

CRISIS

Ruby with family

Ruby at Loyola University New Orleans

Chapter 8

My father got down on one knee. "I pray to the Virgin Mary ... I want you to be a good girl ... I don't care what those college boys tell you. You just stick to your guns." Patrons of the private restaurant in Beaumont ate away at their meals, not noticing Daddy on one knee, holding my hand and looking in my eyes. It is ironic that he spoke this way since Daddy himself was a "skirt-chaser." At any rate, Daddy didn't have anything to worry about. I was not going to lose my virginity at school. A new person was on my horizon though. From one Honduran/Mexican family came a tall, swarthy Latin who would win my heart.

"Why did you divorce Pio, Ruby?" Gamme bent forward a little, truly curious. It was 1991. I could talk and walk again by that time. I looked across the coffee table at Pio's mother. "I guess it was because of his lack of communication."

"I can understand that, " she said knowingly. We mothers have a weakness for our sons. In them we build up our egos and in them we envision men who hold all the good attributes which their Daddies lacked. Mothers can have maternal crushes on their sons; just the way Daddy had a paternal crush on me when he got down on his knee and implored me not to "listen to those college boys."

These kinds of ego crushes create the animosity between mother-in-law and daughter-in-law; father-in-law and son-in-law. But there was never any animosity between Gamme and me now.

"Since you have asked me that question Gamme, I feel free to ask you another question. Why did you say you were never going to speak to me again when I divorced Pio?"

Gamme blinked once and then looked away, past me. "I don't know," she said. She sipped at her coffee. Pio shared this same attribute with Gamme. Neither one of them ever wanted to deal with the important issues. They were both repressed.

Following the divorce, Gamme had not spoken to me for two years. Then I was shot. Upon seeing me in bed at Baptist Hospital, with the bullet wound in my face, probably something moved in her heart.

Through the haze of shock, brain damage, and pain killers, I had seen Gamme standing above my bed. She had brought me a nightgown and had spoken to me. At the time, I hadn't been able to respond. It wasn't until later, when my consciousness was turning back on, that I realized how important Gamme's actions had been that day by my hospital bed.

Over the years of my physical rehabilitation and spiritual transformation, I saw Gamme from time to time. Once I got my voice back, I started walking to her house once a week with my cane and foot brace and prismed glasses. We became friends. And now finally, Gamme and I had asked the questions which we had always needed to ask each other. The hatchet was finally buried. The person on both of our minds during this visit was her only son and my only husband. He turned in both our heads in different, yet similar ways.

"Tell me about your background Gamme." I didn't call her "Old Lady" anymore. That was Pio's playful nickname for his mother which he had gotten all of us to call her. But then he had gotten the children to call me "The Hag." That didn't seem so playful.

"Why, Ruby?" She didn't call me "the Hag" anymore. Pio was and is a very playful person, full of play and mirth. Calling his mother "Old Lady" and his wife "The Hag" to him was all in good fun and got everyone to laugh. I laughed, too, thinking I should just go along and so I also called Gamme "Old Lady."

Back then, I wanted to be just like everyone else. That is until I woke up from my adolescence and saw life and passion and how I had missed so much by being too acquiescent to him. So I told Pio to stop calling me "the Hag." I wasn't ever a hag. And it wasn't funny. While we were still married, I went back to school and graduated with my Masters Degree in Social Work.

I still wouldn't have divorced him had Pio just opened up and dealt with his manipulation and his repressed feelings and his sarcastic shield. Maybe it was because Pio had never had a Daddy. But Pio couldn't open up. And that was the reason I ended our twenty years together. I tightened my grip on my cane remembering that moment in time when I had decided to leave.

"I want to understand him. I want to understand what he came from." Gamme leaned back in her chair. She said her Daddy had come from Mexico and his name was Jose Ortiz Monasterio. He had been a general in the Mexican army during their Civil War and his side had lost. So they had been forced to flee the country and come to New Orleans around 1917 or 1920.

While in New Orleans, her father, General Monasterio, had gotten a job as a professor of Mathematics at Loyola University. He and his wife had five children. Gamme remembered when her brother died and everyone had to wear black for a year. They lived in an apartment on Calhoun Street by Audubon Park. I don't know how Gamme met her husband, Jorge Alfredo Bertot, but somehow they eloped. Alfredo was in New Orleans going to Dental School at Loyola so I guess there must have been some connection between the her father, the General, and Alfredo.

Alfredo was the product of a widower and a widow who had remarried each other in La Ceiba, Honduras. Alfredo was their only child. Anyhow, I don't know how Alfredo and Gamme got back to La Ceiba, Honduras, but they did. He and Gamme were married there and she was no longer a Monasterio but became a Bertot.

La Ceiba, Honduras, was where Pio was born in 1936. Gamme and Alfredo went back to New Orleans after some time (I'm not sure how long) and had two more children (two girls). Alfredo settled into a dental practice in Covington, Louisiana, which is a suburb of New Orleans across Lake Pontchartrain.

After some time, Alfredo wanted to go back to La Ceiba, Honduras, and start a dental practice there. When he left the States, he told Gamme he would send for her and the children but he never did. In La ceiba, Alfredo fell into drinking. His extended family took care of him for the rest of his life.

Pio's real name by the way is also Jorge Alfredo Bertot after his Daddy. But ever since was in his Momma's womb, his nickname had been "Pio" which comes from the Spanish children's rhyme that Gamme had sung to him which repeats, "Pio, Pio, Pio ... " and a bunch of other words in Spanish. But I don't know Spanish but I know "Pio" means something like "little bird."

The last time Pio ever saw his real father was when he was in boarding school. Alfredo must have been visiting New Orleans. He came to Pio's school and asked his little boy if he'd like to come with him to get some lunch. Pio had said "No" because he was afraid.

After Alfredo left, Gamme met a man eight years younger than she was. Irving Louria Lyons, Jr. or "Nicky" Lyons, as we called him, was a very unique person. A gifted pianist, he had graduated from Julliard University at the age of sixteen. Nicky Lyons came from a wealthy family who owned a big drug distribution company with outlets around the South.

He married Gamme and they had two more children; again girls. During the war, Nicky moved Gamme and all the children to Galveston, Texas. It was at this time, that Nicky adopted Pio and gave Pio his last name. Jorge Alfredo Bertot became Pio Lyons. Also during this time, Gamme herself became a naturalized citizen. She had never been a U.S. citizen up until then.

After the war, they returned to New Orleans and Nicky took over his family's business. He was doing very well. Nicky increased the number of branches throughout the south. But one day, he showed up for a board meeting wearing a top hat and tails. Gamme in hindsight says she knew something was wrong before that board meeting but it didn't dawn on her that Nicky was mentally ill. Now when she looked back on it Gamme could see the signs but at the time, in the early 50s, she hadn't been able to see what was happening.

Gamme put Nicky into a mental institution. He came out six weeks later feeling fine and on medication. When Nicky took his medication, he was fine but when he didn't, all hell broke loose. Nicky was diagnosed as a paranoid schizophrenic.

They stayed married for a total of ten years. But at the end, Gamme couldn't handle Nicky. They divorced in the early 50s.

At the end of his life, Nicky was driving a cab. Or so I'm told. I've never met him. I understand Nicky didn't have a tooth in his head. Schizophrenia does terrible things especially if you have it and deny it.

Ranny used to smoke a lot. He said he used cigarettes to unblock his heart arteries. To try to unblock one's heart arteries with cigarettes is crazy. Plus, heart trouble runs in our family. Not surprisingly, in 1982, when he was fifty years old, Ranny had a heart attack, but recovered.

When he came down to New Orleans and helped me in 1984 he was very weak. That year, I rode in my wheelchair in the New Orleans Crescent City Classic. Ranny could hardly walk the few blocks from my house to watch the race. His condition worsened until he needed to have a bypass in early 1985. The doctors gave him a blood transfusion during the bypass. The blood the doctor's used had not been screened for Hepatitis C and Ranny caught the disease.

After the bypass, Ranny became very ill but they didn't know what was wrong so he went to a diagnostic hospital in Houston. There they told him he had contracted Hepatitis C. They said that he could live but that he mustn't drink alcohol again. His condition worsened while at the hospital. I heard my favorite sibling was ill so two of my children took me to Houston to see Ranny. He had turned yellow with bad jaundice. The doctors said that Ranny would pull out of his condition but he kept getting worse.

When I went in and saw him, Ranny looked very bad. He was having trouble with numbers. He couldn't figure the amount of calories in his foods. His problems reminded me of my own disability. I didn't think he was dying. I didn't want to think he was dying. I pretended everything would be alright and he would come back to New Orleans and stay with his sleeping bag on the floor of my house.

After the shooting, Ranny had always come to my house and looked after me. He'd sleep right in the front living room on the hard wood floor. I knew better than to ask him to sleep on a couch or on a bed. Ranny was more comfortable on the floor. He was a very humble man, probably a discipline left over from his days as a monk.

Ranny was so appreciative of beauty. He taught me that you could see and admire beauty but you could never posses it.

My children and I left the hospital and went to stay with our family in Beaumont. The next day Ranny went into intensive care and a few days later he died. After Ranny's death, I'd find myself speaking to him, or praying to his spirit at least two or three times a day. I still find things in the world everyday that remind me of Ranny.

*

I got a call one day in the middle of my Freshmen year of college.
I was at Immaculata and one of the girls came into my room and
told me I had a phone call on our communal telephone line. I
answered and it was Pio Lyons. He told me we had sat next to one
another in English class. That didn't seem right to me since no boy
had sat next to me in English class. I told him I doubted he was
telling the truth and Pio laughed, "Alright, maybe I'm fibbing. One
of your friends gave me this number and told me to ask for you.
She said I ought to call you up."

I thought about it. I wasn't sure I liked getting a random call from
a boy, of course, it depended on how he looked. He told me he was
an architect, or studying architecture at Tulane University and that
he had just designed a church's communion rail. Would I like to go
to the church and see the rail on Sunday? I said, alright.

The next Sunday Pio was to pick me up in the afternoon and
we were to go to the church. I remember it was December 8th
because that is the Day of the Immaculate Conception. I thought
I might miss a special ceremony at Immaculata for the Day of the
Immaculate Conception so I called Pio's house to cancel the date.
Gamme answered the phone and said that Pio had already left to
meet me. So I was stuck going on the date.

Pio turned out to be very interesting. He smoked a pipe which I
found to be mature and sophisticated. I was also impressed that
Pio would soon be an architect since Ranny had also studied
architecture. I think Pio found me to be a very funny girl. I said the
word "alligator" with my Texan accent and he loved it, laughing at
me. After the date we didn't kiss. In fact, I rarely kissed the boys

I went out with. Pio dropped me off at Immaculata and I went inside. Though I wasn't in love with Pio, he was a nice boy, very interesting.

As the weeks and months went by, Pio and I occasionally talked to one another. We could only meet once every six weeks or so for a date since Pio was very busy with school, so Pio became more mysterious for me. His swarthy Latin complexion was appealing. When we were together, I knew that at that moment I was involved with a person whose time was very valuable.

Though he was just a poor college boy, (I don't think the Lyons family helped Gamme or Nicky's old family much after she divorced him), in my eyes Pio's worth began to climb. I loved that he was Latin and different from all the other boys. He was very sarcastic and funny and in control and I wanted to get closer to him.

Five months passed and then one day in May as my Freshman year of college was coming to an end, Pio and I went on a date. We went out to Lake Pontchartrain and by the lake shore, Pio leaned over toward me. I could tell he wanted to kiss me. I backed away a little. "If you want to kiss me, are you going to marry me?"

"Okay, sure, Ruby, I'll marry you." He said, touching my arm.

It was a very, very nice kiss. Afterward, the bond was tied between us. Neither of us said anything about that conversation but after that day I stopped seriously dating other boys. I still dated but it was only in friendship and I didn't kiss another boy while Pio and I were courting.

*

As the rehabilitation started to work, I wanted to exercise more. I had an old adult tricycle that I used to pull my kids around with when they were very young. I thought it would be a good idea to use the tricycle again in order to be more mobile and independent. I thought using a tricycle would be easier for me because I wouldn't have to balance myself on it.

I had a handyman take the tricycle out of storage and get it ready for me to ride. The handyman put the bike out in the yard. One day, when I was alone I pushed the tricycle to the sidewalk and got on. I was planning on going to the park and meeting Mary Jane.

When I got on the bike I felt free. I was by myself and riding along. Then right at the curb as I was turning my bike, I couldn't shift my weight and the bike toppled over. I fell flat on my left side and the fall knocked the wind out of me. I lay there on the ground gasping for breath when this nice young man came by and helped me up. He told me he, too, had a stroke. Everyone in my neighborhood knew I had been shot and had a stroke.

After that close call, Mary Jane and I decided a better way for me to travel around was with her. I decided to purchase a bicycle built for two which worked well. I used it often with Mary Jane and even some of my children pedaled me around on it.

It was a relief knowing that somebody else was driving the bike. I got to pump hard behind and move quickly around the neighborhood. Riding was freeing to a certain point, however I still depended on someone to take me for a ride.

I kept on using the bike for about six months. Then one day Mary Jane came over to take me out to Audubon park. We got on the bike and about a block away from the park we went over a bump in the road. Since I am semi-paralyzed I can't easily shift my weight. Mary Jane told me as we went over the bump that my weight was like a heavy sack of potatoes. She couldn't control the bike and we toppled over.

I landed again on my side. Again the fear. Was I hurt? Would I have more suffering, more pain? I had a world of pain already and I didn't want anymore. I was done with pain. I had no fear of death because I had come so close to it. But the idea of more pain was terrible. Mary Jane pushed the bike off of us and sat me up. I was alright but I knew I couldn't ride the bike again, not after falling twice.

I have fallen a few more times since then. Most of the falls haven't been a problem. One time, however I fell at a clothing store and broke my shoulder. This was a few years ago. The pain was horrible. I was conscious for every second.

Pio visited Beaumont in the summer of 1958 after my Freshmen year of school. To my family and my father, Pio was always soft-spoken and polite. He was really a very shy person who was withdrawn and hard to get to know. It was only among our peers that his sarcasm came out. Pio would use his sarcasm to keep other people at bay and to maintain control of a social situation. Of course, he was not, and is not, conscious of his behavior. If you asked him, he would say, "No, I don't do anything like that!"

It was interesting to see my family's response to me bringing home a Mexican. Though my family was Catholic and felt a religious empathy toward other Catholics (i.e. Latin people), we were still very American. There was a demarcation between Americans and Latins. They weren't fully accepted. They were like Blacks but better, a notch above. But even one of Pio's sisters was asked to sit at the back of a street car with the black people during the 1950s. Latins weren't always a notch above in the South.

I remember one Sunday lunch during Pio's first visit to Beaumont. We were all sitting out on the porch waiting for the meal to be served when Daddy's Daddy, Big Tom said in the middle of a conversation about Mexicans, "'Ain't much to them Mexicans." Pio and I immediately looked at each other. Texans tend to say simple things but their coarse words have a lot of meaning. There wasn't much we could say, we just shrugged our shoulders at each other. No one said anything about Pio being Mexican but everyone knew.

And yet at the same time, they seemed not to fully count Pio as a Mexican American. Pio had gone to decent schools and he was a Catholic. He spoke like we did (well, he spoke like a New Orleanian and we spoke like Texans but we were all well-spoken at the end of the day).

We Whites in Texas, and all over America, wanted to be better than somebody. We wanted to feel superior and secure so we looked down on Latins, Blacks, and Asians. It was all just a game of ego. It is not just Whites who play the ego game of racial prejudice. I'll give you an example, me.

Since the shooting, people haven't viewed me as a White woman, at least not when they first meet me. Now they see me first as DISABLED and this prejudice cuts across all races. I can be in a Black neighborhood and I can come across a prejudiced person but he or she almost always sees me first as disabled before seeing my skin color.

This prejudice about disabled people has allowed me to have an immediate connection with almost all people. Even though humanity tends to hold a prejudice about disabled people, this prejudice has worked to my advantage. For a few seconds I think that people forget their egos when they see me.

*

Besides helping me go out and do things, Mary Jane (who was a big Catholic just as I used to be) made sure to take me to church daily after she got off of her job at Charity Hospital as a Medical Technologist.

When I first got back to New Orleans from TIRR, I didn't know how to respond to church. As my shock began to wear off and my mental and physical rehabilitation improved, I began to feel more independent. Not independent enough yet to make any big decisions but different questions began to form in my mind.

During my shock period (July 16, 1983 until late 1985) my mental and spiritual capacities were totally involved with healing. I kept wanting to get back to "where I had been before." I was in absolute denial about what had happened to me. As two years passed my denial and shock lessened. I began to realize that these problems weren't going to just go away. My life had been totally changed and I didn't know why.

Can you explain it? One day a person is alive and well and then is cut down? Why?

The more I thought about it, the angrier I became. I couldn't be angry at the robbers because they were gone. After the shooting, the police had shown me pictures and asked me if I recognized anyone who looked like the boys who had shot me. I couldn't give an honest answer. It had all happened so fast and I couldn't remember what the boys looked like.

There was no way to be sure who had shot me and blaming someone just to make myself feel better would have been very wrong, so I kept telling the police I couldn't identify the boys' faces. To this day, I truly can't remember what they looked like.

Who had shot me? I didn't really know. Had it been God?

Since I had no other "one" to blame, I began to get angry with God. It must have been God and Jesus who had shot me that day when earlier in the park during my jog I had entreated Jesus to give me suffering. And there was no doubt He had given it to me!

I would compare myself with Jesus. At least, he had died. I, on the other hand, was cursed to live in this prison of a body. I tried not to think like this too often (but more and more often, it would become unavoidable).

*

I completed my major in Philosophy at Loyola and also finished two years of school at Tulane for my minor in Psychology. All told, I had finished everything in three years of school, graduating a year early. At that time, I had the chance to go to Europe.

However, I wasn't aching to leave the United States. Once I was done with school my plan was to marry (back then you were an old maid if you weren't married by age twenty-five) and settle down in Boulder, Colorado and have "issues." Pio wanted to get married but he had to do his military service first. Back then, we had the draft and almost all the young men went and served in the military after college.

As Pio finished his school and I finished mine, I realized that I would have at least six months free to myself. Momma had told me that Pio needed to have a job before we could marry and since he was going into the military right out of school there was no way he could get a job before that.

Pio and I promised to marry when he got back from the Army but until then I was on my own. I didn't know what to do. Some friends and relatives urged me to go to Europe and study in Vienna. One of my cousins told me about an amazing Austrian Jewish Professor named Viktor Frankl.

I was on the fence post. I had the typical inferiority complex of women. It was 1960 and I thought of myself as subservient to my soon-to-be-husband. So you see, not all of what would happen between Pio and me was his fault. I, in fact, had a lot of blame.

Well, since everyone said I ought to check out Europe, I went on a college exchange program to Vienna. I remember on the boat, they gave us a blank piece of construction paper and told us to draw the continent of Europe and mark and name the capitals of each country. I just wasn't passionate about Europe. I sure am now! It is amazing how much people can change, how much we can transform ourselves in this lifetime, readying for the next.

My group and I arrived in Europe. My first night in Europe I
was scared, scared the way I had been during my first week of
university. I knew just what to do. I went to sleep and the next day
things were better.

We traveled about Europe and made our way down to Vienna.
And in that windswept, snow blown land I met and listened to the
great Dr. Viktor Frankl. I'll write more about Dr. Frankl later. For
me, I really felt free and I was learning a new language and a new
culture. Post-War Vienna had a beauty combined with destruction.
A part of me very much wanted to stay.

After six months, Pio got out of the army and we talked on the
phone. I told him I wasn't sure I was ready to come home yet. I told
him I might stay in Europe a bit more. He was young and in love
and wanted to get married, "Okay. Well, then how about I come
and visit you?" I felt something sink in my chest. Pio couldn't come
here to Vienna. It wasn't right for him to be here with me. If he
came, we would break up. Was he challenging me? Or did he just
love me? Or both? "No, no Pio. I'll come home. I'll come home."
And I did.

*

I began to wonder about Dr. Frankl's message as I woke up from the
shooting. I would sit wondering about Dr. Frankl and remember.
His classroom had been very stark, with no feeling. It was very cold
in the school. I had looked forward to Dr. Frankl's class. He was
always teaching me something I didn't know. I really admired him.
He had gone through a lot of suffering and he had the right attitude.

Being Jewish, Dr. Frankl was put in a German concentration camp
during World War II. He explained that he had used a broken piece

of glass to shave with every day so that he would appear healthy. Though he was starving and bone thin, he conducted himself with dignity. He had a will to his life. He conceived of it and he made it his, even in the concentration camp.

At one point, Dr. Frankl had sewn a book manuscript about his theory of life — Logotherapy — into the insides of a long coat he wore. The German guards had discovered the manuscript and destroyed it and his coat in front of him. I was moved to tears when I heard this story. I couldn't believe that someone had suffered so much and still lived to tell about it. Dr. Frankel had lost his mother, father and wife in the concentration camps.

Dr. Frankl felt that even in horrible conditions, life has potential meaning and that because of this possibility for potential meaning, suffering is very important. Finally, Frankl believed that how we deal with suffering creates meaning in our lives.

As I sat in that cold classroom listening to Dr. Frankel, I reflected on my life and the huge role suffering had for me growing up as a Catholic. I think I began to conceive of a world where guilt and suffering were not linked. I began for a few months to be guilt-free.

It was odd to be in Vienna at that time. Everything was so poor and much of the city was still bombed out from World War II. In the winter, men would light fires in garbage cans. The wind came out of Siberia and froze everything. Even the holy water in the Cathedral where I went for my daily mass was frozen like pomade. We would rub the ice in the holy water font and slather our wet finger tips on our foreheads. Everyone had a distant look to them.

There were few children around. It was almost as if the world itself was too sad and austere for the happy cries of children running in the streets. The Viennese had dogs, though. They could take them on street cars, take them anywhere. The dogs seemed to be their substitute for their lack of children. All the people in Vienna seemed to dress in blacks, navy blues, and forest greens. I never saw a Viennese smile or anything. Their faces on the buses were stoic and expressionless. You almost felt as if they unconsciously hated you and you didn't know why.

It was right after the war and the occupation of Vienna had just ended a few years earlier. Also it was winter. But all that aside, I really wanted to make people smile when they saw me.

I was learning German (five days a week) and I made sure to wear bright pinks and reds and lavenders. I always smiled at them and said hello like a polite Texan girl.

But all of my efforts were to no avail. No one ever said hello back. The Viennese were very hard to get to know. They weren't anything like back home in Beaumont or New Orleans. I thought that even Yankees were more friendly than Viennese.

The Viennese seemed scared of anything unknown. It was an odd way to live. I could watch people but it was very difficult to talk to anyone. They all had a far away look in their eyes and without knowing it they were afraid and in denial.

In the Austrian and German history books of that time, they didn't even write anything about World War II or Nazis. They all were trying to erase something they had all shared and was constantly in their minds. No one spoke about World War II.

The school children never heard a thing about it from their teachers and most often, not from their parents either.

All that aside, I was beginning to see the beauty of Vienna. The old buildings, the cobble stone streets, the food (especially the apple strudel and knerdals). I would walk daily from my little apartment around the corner to the Cathedral for mass. Then I would walk into the old city, to the Poly Clinic with all of its old buildings and enter my university courses.

Dr. Frankl was becoming a mentor for me. He included spiritual belief as an integral part of his "will to meaning" because he felt that spiritual belief could help people in their quest for meaning. This resonated with me because I was such a Catholic.

When I returned home in 1961 I reverted back to my old Catholic self. I didn't know how to get rid of my guilt and suffering. Dr. Frankl's concept of suffering was different than what I had been raised with but after I returned home I didn't think much about the difference.

Now that I was shot, I thought anew about Dr. Frankl's idea of suffering. As my consciousness grew, I began to wonder about Victor Frankl Had he been all the way right about suffering and had I been all the way wrong? I'm an extreme person and this is how I think. I couldn't see any point in suffering anymore.

In fact, I asked the Goddess that I was beginning to believe in to not give me any more pain. I didn't want to suffer. Why had I been shot? While running on that final day, why had I thought it necessary to ask to suffer? Had God misunderstood me? What about all that need to find meritorious suffering? How did that fit in with Frankl's ideas on suffering? All of these questions came out of a time (about a year and half after the shooting in early 1985) when I still couldn't read and mentally I felt like I was demented or retarded. I was afraid I would end up in a home.

I thought about Dr. Frankl and the frigid winter in Vienna. Besides in class, I would see Dr. Frankl on Sundays as I left the Cathedral. He sat in a café across the street waiting for his wife. He had remarried since the war. His new wife was Catholic and went to the same church that I did. Dr. Frankl waited in the café for her. I would go to the café and watch them together. He always stood up and hugged her when she came to the table after mass. I was amazed that he could be happy again after losing everything.

Don't think for a second that I regret marrying Pio. He was the father of my children and I'd never, ever exchange having my children. They are the most precious things in my life. Pio also loves his kids. He is good to them. In my next life though, I don't want to be a parent or a spouse. I want to stay in Europe or wherever.

Pio's and my wedding happened on the 29th of May, 1961, in Beaumont, Texas. It was on a washday. We both look very young in the pictures because we were. I look at Pio as if I was very in love with him because I was. Pio appears shy. I call it my shotgun wedding because there were so few guests.

Pio had just gotten an architecture job in Denver and we were readying to move to Boulder. But first, of course, the wedding.

After the wedding, Pio and I flew up to Denver for our honeymoon. That first night I was so scared. Momma and I had never had that

"Mother and Daughter" talk but from my roommates, I knew what was going to happen and I figured it was going to hurt a lot. I was so frightened that I thought about running out of the hotel room. I asked Pio, "Why don't we just give it up to the Lord tonight and consummate our marriage tomorrow morning?" Pio said, "Okay, Ruby." And we went to sleep.

The next morning, Pio woke me. He wanted to have sex. I acquiesced. It hurt a little bit. I was so disappointed because I didn't feel any emotion. It was like we were both under pressure. I guess there was some romantic feeling but mostly we just wanted to get it over with. Afterward, I didn't know what to do with the sperm inside of me. I'd never even thought about what to do with sperm. I ran to the bathroom and put in a tampon, so that the sperm wouldn't flow out and get all over.

Eight months and three weeks later, our first-born child came into the world. My sister Peggy called from the convent to point out the fact that the pregnancy had not been a full nine months from the wedding. But then again she was in a convent.

We moved to Boulder, Colorado, and Pio would commute to work everyday. The Boulder of my girlhood and the real Boulder were two very different places. I was bored and the people there just didn't seem that friendly. After only six weeks, Pio and I decided to move back to New Orleans. Though I had tried to avoid the city, New Orleans felt more like home than any other place. We moved into a basement apartment and Pio went and found a new architecture job.

After our first child was born, my Momma came to New Orleans and fell in love with the baby. Though Momma had been hesitant to accept Pio as a son-in-law, all that was changed as she bonded with this new grandchild, Tom. My Momma was "Momma Toots" to her grandchildren and because I was a mother, Momma looked at me as an adult now.

It was 1962 and the world was beginning to change. We were young. Pio talked about buying a new house soon. I wanted more babies to fill up the house. Though I had played with breaking from the mold when I was in Vienna, now that time and that world abroad was a distant land; a different life.

It was 1962. I was a housewife and finally, a mother.

Chapter 9

In 1971, I had my fifth child, a miracle. Pio and I had practiced the Rhythm Method for our first four years of marriage. It worked wonderfully ... after three children in four years, I switched to the Pill. It made me very sick. My body was allergic to it. I would have a headache and dizzy spells. I was even forced to stay in bed one day out of every month because the symptoms were so debilitating. On that day, I couldn't do anything, no cooking, no carpools, no help with homework, I was really sick.

Why couldn't Pio and the other men have taken a male Pill? Why did we women have to shove hormones into our bodies and play with our natural levels? Was it because we were traditionally the "hysterical ones"?

Anyway, after two years of the Pill, I couldn't take it anymore and I switched to Foam. The Foam worked well till one night I forgot to put it in. Nine months later, our fourth child was born. That was in 1969. We kept on with the Foam after the fourth child and then came the miracle, our last baby. Even though we were using the Foam, I became pregnant for a fifth time. I don't know how that sperm got through.

After the fifth child in nine years, I stopped wanting to have children. Six weeks before the birth of our third child, my bladder fell out. It felt like having a grapefruit between my legs. After the birth, the bladder miraculously popped back into place. In fact, I was in the hospital recovering when my bladder went back into place. A doctor came by my bed with a group of medical students and opened my legs, shoving his finger in my vagina and saying to the students, "This woman is amazing! Her bladder actually popped back up into place!"

A few years later, six weeks pregnant with my fourth child, my bladder popped out again. By the way, when I say "my bladder popped out," I mean that it lowered into my uterus and it would have fallen out of me had it not been for the uterus. Anyhow, the doctors put a very uncomfortable pessary into me. It was one of the old hard plastic pessaries. Did it ever hurt going in!

I bled some. When it was finally in place, my bladder was supported and I felt much better.

During the pregnancies of my fourth and fifth children, the pessary stayed inside of me. After the birth of my fifth child, I didn't want anymore children and I didn't want to use the pessary any longer. I asked the doctor for a hysterectomy. I was only 32. The hysterectomy was a very easy procedure but it left me alienated. It was an odd feeling. I could no longer have babies. Also, I had gained some weight from my last pregnancy. I couldn't lose it. I wasn't sure what to do.

Right around that time, one of Pio's architecture clients, the C.E.O. of Burger King, told me about a new fad. The interesting thing about this man wasn't that he was some big-wig, but that he was half Indian and half white ... and all gorgeous. He told me about this new health craze all over California called jogging. He said that when people jogged they ran just to stay healthy. So I decided to try it.

In the middle of the day I would give my two youngest children (the older three were already in school) to a neighborhood girlfriend and I would run around the block. The first day, I could barely run half a block. I wore my Baker's tennis shoes and I was slow. But I went back and did it the next day. I was determined to lose weight. So I did it the next day and the next. And the next. And people would stop and ask me if I needed help. Was there a fire? Should they call the police? I would look over my shoulder and smile and say, "No, I'm just jogging!" I started to have a great time.

With these first runs, I was gaining a focus on my life. My heart beat was steady. I was breathing in and out now. Breathing in and out ... but as I ran, I began to realize I was emotionally dependent on my husband, Pio, was distant. I see now that he was like Momma all over again; putting a box around me and protecting me but unable to love. I became dependent on a man just the way Momma had been dependent on Daddy.

During the week, I would tell Pio once or twice that I loved him but he never told me that he loved me. I would do what he told me to do. I cooked, cleaned, mended shirts, weeded, did gardens, took care of the children, gave haircuts, ran carpools. He would call in the evening wanting to be sure the children were all fed.

Though my children might remember it differently I have a hard time remembering a time when Pio ate with us, his family. He was always sitting in a separate room, eating and drinking while I sat at the table with the kids, eating their leftovers.

Friday nights were Pio's night to be free and go to the French Quarter with his friends. All the men went out for dinner and watched music and I stayed at home. I made dinner for myself and the children and then went to bed.

On Saturdays, Pio would take his boat out to the Gulf of Mexico and go fishing with his friends. I didn't see him much on the weekends. I didn't see him much at all when the children were small.

One time, I was very stressed with the task of having the five children all to myself to raise and I insisted to Pio that he had to at least listen to me. I wanted to share what had happened with our kids that day. We were laying in bed and he was slowly getting sick of my "whining." Eventually, he stood up out of bed, got dressed and said, "I'm leaving." And out the door he went.

I ran after him and caught him at the front door and spun him around and slapped him on the face and shouted, "You will listen to me Pio!" That time he listened. A few months later, I got angry at his absence again and slapped him a second time. This time his eyes got a funny look and he just quietly said without raising his hand, "If you ever do that again, Ruby, I'm out of here." There was the threat. He'd leave me with the five kids. At least, that is the way it sounded to me.

All the same, I should have never hit him. For that, I was wrong. What is anger? I think about Momma. She and Daddy split in the late 60s. Ten years or so later, she finally gave him a divorce so he could marry a new woman. Momma felt as if she hadn't done anything with her life. She didn't count having children as doing something valuable.

One time, Momma was complaining about a relative that she didn't like. Suddenly, she broke down and said to me, "Oh, Ruby, I haven't done anything with my life. Not like you!"

Momma was angry with HERSELF but that is how anger is. Anger really has nothing to do with how other people act. We feel anger at ourselves. We have a desire that the world and people around us be a certain way. But that is all desire is ... just a creation of our ego. Our ego has a desire and ego wants its desire to occur in order to feel satisfaction. So we run after that satisfaction. We hope others will help us feel good. But this is a lie.

The moment we define ourselves on what other's think, we are being adolescent and afraid. When the world isn't as we want it to be, we feel anger and pain. But this is a lie, too. It is part of ego. The key is to leave ego aside, to see all of the desires and unhealthiness of our egos and leave all that aside, too. And then we can do so much.

Ultimately, we are angry at our situations and at ourselves for having the "wrong" response. Our egos and our minds create desires but the world doesn't meet those desires. The frustration of that is anger. We are angry at ourselves for this situation. I had no person to blame for my shooting. Since there was no one to be angry at I was very angry at God.

During the 60s, I was happy because I was busy having children. All through my life, I had put my worth in myself based on what other people thought of me. During the 60s, I based my worth on what kind of mother I was.

By the early 1970s, Pio and I had entered "polite" New Orleans society. Pio and I got to know quite a few famous politicians, businessmen, and Catholic clergy. I see now that I was very repressed then. I had reverted back to being like my mother and I looked to others for my own self-esteem. I was immature; I was in a prolonged adolescence. It is hard to wake up. That big word "adult" didn't have much meaning. After adolescence, we are all physically adults. The issue is waking up, living an awake, alive life.

*

All of the counter-culture seeds sprung loose and grew wild in America during the 1960s. Everything which society had repressed in my childhood was being questioned and reexamined. Suddenly women were awake and focused on their bodies and themselves. People began to meditate and learn about other cultures and realize how inferior the Western World was.

This new America grew out of California. California was the place where the new and bold grew and blew into greater America.

I would walk into Audubon Park with my children pulling a child's wagon. Audubon Park is the large park in the Uptown section of New Orleans. It is named after famous New Orleanian, John James Audubon. Audubon Park is a bit like a mini-New York Central Park only with tropical flora and fauna.

The children and I used to love to walk by St. Charles Avenue around a large oak tree. That oak is still there. The boughs of the tree bend down low to the ground. We would sit down there and have a picnic! Afterward, we would go to the fountain and the children would wade in the water.

It was during those times that the Hippies were having their nationwide "Love-ins." On those days, I would take the kids out with me and we would give the college students who sat in the park (the hippies) crepe paper flowers which my children and other neighborhood children had made. It was around this time, the early 70s, that I started to call myself an Uptown Christian Hippie.

After I got good at running, I would wake up at 5:30 in the morning everyday for a run. I would leave the house, with my husband, Pio, fast asleep in our bed and my children snoring away. I was out breathing the cool morning air. I would run into Audubon Park at dawn. At that early time of the morning, Mayor Moon Landreiu, had closed the park to traffic. This made the park more beautiful and easier to run in. Running had helped me lose the weight I wanted to. I looked good and I was happy.

About that time, I read an article in a national Catholic newspaper about Zen. The article was titled "Zen Mind and the Bible." I was really interested so I asked a friend if they knew of anyone who did Zen and that was how I first heard about Father Ben Wren, the Zen priest.

Ben was a tall, half-Japanese, half-Portuguese man, 6´5˝ and most people called him "Big Ben" after the "Big Bird" on Sesame Street. But to us, his students, we would call him, "Ben Wren, the Zen." Ben was a Jesuit priest who taught history at Loyola University. I saw him one day when I was jogging through Audubon Park sitting under an oak tree, propped up on the tree's roots. Ben always sat in the lotus position, his closed eyes shaped like crescent Buddha smiles.

As I approached him, Ben was chanting "Jesus Christ" quietly, totally absorbed.

I squatted on the knotted oak tree roots next to him. "Hi, Ben Wren, my name is Ruby Lyons and I've heard about you. Would you teach me everything you know about Zen?"

Ben's face folded into a frown. He opened his eyes, "I was meditating," he replied.

How did I know for sure it was Ben Wren the Zen and not some other stranger in the park? Well, in New Orleans there wasn't a good chance that a 6´5˝ half-Japanese half-Portuguese man would be sitting in the lotus position in the park meditating if it wasn't Ben. I apologized to him for my disruption. He nodded taciturnly. "Alright, I'll teach you."

It would turn out that I would be one of Ben's first students. We began our meditation in the basement of the Loyola Student Union.

Zen combined with my running opened me up to a whole new world. As Ben said, the instant we are born we are dead and we are all as different as grains of sand. I learned to take a deep breath to get calm. Ben Wren the Zen pointed out the futility of life. And so. So-so-so. Meditation is a kind of living death but without the negativity or the fear. It is a juxtaposition of the nothingness. I don't know how to describe it. I feel tired just thinking about it.

*

By early 1986, I was going with Mary Jane to church out of rote. The thing that got me the worst was the singing. I used to love to sing and be a part of the mass but now I was on the outside. I could just sit there and look down. My words were coming easier now and I could read but I still couldn't sing.

In fact I've never been able to sing since the shooting. I can carry a tune like "Happy Birthday" but advanced music like spirituals are impossible.

I would sit in the pew while the rest of the congregation sang and feel a numbness growing inside. I felt very low. I would never be what I had been before, what I had envisioned of myself. The people there sang on and on. I kept my eyes on the ground. It was at these times that I could have cried but I pushed on and was a good trooper. I wanted to hide my feelings from everyone, even Mary Jane. I was so ashamed.

Before the shooting, I was planning on helping other people who were going to die. But here I was: not dead, but still not living the way I wanted to.

*

I had never had an orgasm until after my children were born. Like many women in my generation, I didn't know that women could have orgasms. After the children and my hysterectomy, Pio became much more giving in sex. I don't know why exactly but I started having orgasms then. It might have had something to do with me getting more in touch with my body. Also, Pio really was trying harder.

Though the sex had improved, the love and companionship was still lacking. Pio's mysterious, distant ways which had been so appealing when we had first started to date, had become real problems for me in our married life.

I was no longer having kids and I wanted something more to our love life. Actually, I always wanted us to be emotionally closer but for the first 10 years of our marriage I was so busy having children and reverting into my subservient housewife role. Now that I was freer, I wanted a warmth and closeness which Pio didn't seem able to provide. After all my children were born, I began to find that warmth from another man. I let myself kiss him.

Pio certainly wasn't any kind of companion and I was looking for something (in this case, a man) to fill an emptiness I felt inside. I told myself that I needed a real companion to complete myself. And since I wasn't getting that from my own husband, I found it with another man who we were already family friends with.

It was a short affair, if it can even be called an "affair." Now, it would be called an emotional affair. We never had sex, just kissed. He was a handsome man. His name was Pete. I met him when he came to find out about a room for rent on our property. I liked Pete's sense of humor. He made everyone laugh. Being with him, I had a great time. He would take all of us, me and my children, to the Gulf Coast beach and we would just play all day. The water of the Gulf is brown and brackish but we didn't care. It really was nice.

I liked Pete. He had a lot of other girlfriends but he liked me, too. We kissed a few times. Later, I felt bad about what I had done and went to Father Ben for an official Catholic confession. That's right, my Zen instructor was also my confessor priest! So it goes in New

Orleans. Father Ben dispensed forgiveness, giving me prayers to say for penance.

As Pio and I briefly discussed infidelity, and I told him about kissing Pete and other men, and that it was purely innocent. He didn't say a word to me about it. I wanted to always be honest with Pio. I wondered if he honest with me?

✳

After the shooting, people would come up to me after mass as I stood with my cane and comment, "How well I was looking" or "How well I was doing" or "Hadn't I come far!" It was all "putting on the dog." It rang fake to me. Deep down, unconsciously, I think all those old acquaintances were just acting kind to me because of the guilt they felt at seeing me. Most of them wanted to placate their consciences, their egos. I was a reality test for them and most folks didn't want to take the test. They want to feel good about themselves and not see people like me.

These old acquaintances didn't know why they felt guilty when they looked at me and they most of them didn't want to investigate this feeling they were having. I don't know what I wanted from them even to this day. Maybe we all could have gotten used to each other but like I've always done, when it doesn't work for me I make a clean break. Maybe I shouldn't have been so fast in breaking from the Catholic church. ButI had to.

✳

As a child, we used to go to the Chapel Pa-Pa had built into his and Ma-Mee's mansion. On Saturday nights, they would request from each of their three children that they send one of their grandchildren there to be with them. So on Saturday nights, either

Peggy, Ranny, Tommy, Mary, or me would go to the chapel and sit behind Pa-Pa and Ma-Mee with a cousin Uncle Micky sent and a cousin Uncle Bus sent sitting there beside us.

Pa-Pa would say the first prayer on the rosary. He would say it intensely, like a staccato machine gun, sudden and sharp. Then Ma-Mee would read slow and gracious with perfect elocution. They would go back and forth. Pa-Pa would say, "Hailmaryfullofgracethelordiswiththee ..." and then Ma-Mee would continue, "Hail Mary, full of grace, the Lord is with Thee ..." We children would hold in giggles. It was wonderful. The church was very warm. We were all together.

*

Now I was alone in church, alienated. Mary Jane used to take me to mass at Loyola University. Before mass, for my exercise, I would walk a part of the university called the Quadrangle. It is an enclosed courtyard with grass and sidewalks. I would use my cane and walk around the courtyard.

Sometimes a few priests would walk up and greet me. I didn't feel like they were God's helpers anymore. They just wore some robes and a Roman collar and had gone to school to be eventually "consecrated." They weren't blessed or holy or special. No one is. Even the Queen of England makes poo!

I would walk from one end of the Quadrangle to the other. It was here that I felt very, very far from everyone. The grass and the sidewalks and the young university students ran by and I would walk slowly along with my leg in a brace. What was the point? What was the point of any of this?

*

For his part, Pio did make an effort to do a better job as a husband after we talked about infidelity. He started to cook a Sunday night barbecue dinner for the family and during the week he would put his own dishes in the dish washer after dinner. This might not seem like much but it was a big step for Pio. He still kept going fishing on the weekends and he still went out on Friday nights with his friends.

During the late 70s, I began to look deeply into new matters. I was growing away from Pio, little by little, though I still didn't feel as if I could leave him. At the same time, I was curious about other things and people. I wanted very much to learn more about the world. To this end, I began taking night classes on a variety of subjects at my old alma maters Tulane and Loyola Universities.

I learned about the French Jesuit Philosopher de Chardin and his concept of the noosphere. As far as I could understand the noosphere was a place beyond. We can't understand it and we can't go to it except in death. Technically, the noosphere is the void in the sky where the gases of earth end and space has yet to begin.

Ben Wren finally got ecclesiastical permission to teach Zen Meditation as a class at Loyola University and I took his first class. The classes were about the same as the meditation sessions had been. Ben could be very abrupt sometimes. He was always the same. His personality didn't change. And as the years went by Ben became more and more strict about who he would let into the Zen courses. In fact some of the people who had gotten into the Zen course decided not to take it because of Ben's off-putting manner. Ben eventually left the priesthood for a woman he had met while giving his Zen courses. He continued to teach Zen and World History at Loyola until he died.

I spoke to him in 2006 a few months before he died. We talked as old friends. He spoke very softly as he always did. I asked him why he never stopped by my house anymore. He told me that he often had but I was never home.

I still Zazen every morning. From my kitchen window, I look over the trees at the green grass and the birds and squirrels feeding at the nut feeder. The sun shines down around me. Then I walk into my living room and kneel at the couch looking at the ivy tree Ranny had at his funeral. I remember Ranny, Ben Wren, Ron, Momma and Daddy, Tommy, Anne, Baby, and everyone. As I recall their names, I Zazen in my own way, which is different than your way.

My brother, Tommy, was such a character. He would talk tough and "Texas" and never use the right grammatical syntax. That was Tommy's point. He had education but he was a very Texan man and proud of it. My kids loved him. He was their down-home cantankerous "Uncle Tommy."

Tommy ended up inheriting Ma-Mee and Pa-Pa's Texas vacation home which was fifty miles north of Beaumont. I used to take the kids there once a year to see Tommy during the summer. My sister, Mary, would take her kids to see Tommy then, too, and we all had a great time. It was almost like going camping because Tommy kept the place real dirty. He never cleaned. He had a washing machine but no dryer so I hung our clothes out to dry on clotheslines outside of the house.

The kids and I used to help Tommy roll his marijuana joints. He grew the plants in his closet with a blue light. It was funny that we did that. I don't have much to say about pot. I tried it twice. It didn't do anything to me. The first time, I had a brownie with marijuana in it. The second time, I tried smoking it but I didn't inhale. I didn't know how.

I last talked to Tommy on a Monday in May of 1977. He had just gotten a bunch of new birds at his house and he was excited. As we spoke, Tommy said to me, "Ruby, just let your kids do whatever they want. Don't force them into anything!"

Two days later, we learned Tommy had died of a heart attack. The news was sudden and rough. He was the first of my adult siblings to die. He was forty-two years old.

I stopped taking the Zen courses by the late 1970s. I felt like I was meditating already every time I ran in the mornings. Plus, I wanted to do something else besides only night courses. More and more, I was interested in doing something out of the house.

One day in the fall of 1979, my friend, Paula Norris, asked me to come and look at a building that was for rent nearby my house. Paula, a yoga instructor, lived in the neighborhood. We went together to see the building up for rent. It was large enough for our purposes. I was getting the idea to open a shelter for women and Paula wanted to open a center for Yoga instruction. I wanted to call the woman's shelter RAW for Run Away Wives. I was very happy when I went home. I couldn't wait to tell Pio.

When I told him, Pio only grunted, then grimaced and said, "How are you going to get insurance for the building?" then he went back to what he was doing. To be met with such a cold response was shocking. I sat down, feeling hurt for a minute and thought, "Fine. Then I'll just have to go back to school and get my master's degree in Social Work."

*

By early 1986, even though I didn't feel Catholic anymore; I still tried going to mass. I wanted to believe in something. I wanted to connect. It didn't matter what, but I wanted to connect with something. I felt like a nobody. I felt like I had no ties. Who can connect? Nobody knows how another person feels. I had to find the connection on my own.

Even though, I looked everywhere for meaning, the meaning never came. I just wanted to be like everyone else with all their in fact meanings to their lives. I would watch people run from place to place, doing their business and here I was unable to connect with that energy, that essence that they all seemed to have. I was alone.

In the spring of 1986, my friend Margy Ruli and Father One Bun were planning on going to a weekend retreat in Atlanta.

I had known Father One Bun since college. His real name was Father John Keller. He had hip cancer so his entire right leg had to be removed from the hip down. Hence, I had started calling him "Father One Bun" after the amputation. We were friends. I don't know whether or not he liked to be called that by me but I think he got used to it.

I had met Margy Ruli during my Zen classes in the 1970s and we were both looking for alternative spiritualities within the Catholic Church. Margy approached me one day and asked me if I had heard of a very liberal Jesuit priest named Anthony de Mello. She told me about Father de Mello. He was from India. He was supposed to be famous for retreats and for his different views. Other than that, Margy didn't know much about him. She asked me if I would be interested in going along with her to the retreat. I said I would.

There is something I have to admit. I was jealous of Pio, jealous of him for his career. He was and is a damn fine architect. But, of course, I knew I wasn't supposed to feel jealousy for my husband. I should feel proud of my husband's success. However, I was jealous of him and his success. I wanted that success for myself.

For the first year of my Masters work from January 1980 until January 1981, I rode my bicycle to Tulane University twice a week in the evenings. I was used to evening classes because I had taken them over the last ten years. During this first year, Pio didn't seem much phased by my courses because I continued to be a perfect housewife by day. The next year though, I decided to go back to school full time and concentrate completely on finishing my Master's degree.

This decision changed everything. Pio began calling me sometimes three or four times a day when I was in the middle of field work. He would ask me questions about what we were having for dinner and when would I have time to take care of the kids. Slowly, it became impossible to live with him and get my degree. I kept trying to do both. But my degree became more and more important to me.

I went to a Gestalt therapist named Anne Teachworth. I told her I was thinking of divorcing my husband. It was through talks with Anne that I began to understand how unhealthy my relationship with Pio had become. I felt as if I could trust Anne. She was a woman about my age who was divorced with six sons. Here was a peer who had been forced to understand herself in relationship to ALL the men in her life, both young and old, and I felt she could understand the difficulty I was having understanding myself now.

I told Pio that he needed to open up and share with me. I wanted our relationship to be different. I was changing and I needed him to grow with me or I was afraid our relationship would end. We needed to communicate. So Pio went and spoke with Anne once. She told me later that it was a productive session and that Pio almost opened up but then he checked himself and closed down. After that one and only session with Anne, Pio told me, "I'm not going to that therapist anymore, Ruby!"

Calmly, I told Pio, "I'm going to have to divorce you if you won't go to couple therapy with me." He told me he wasn't going and we wasn't giving up the house and wouldn't give me a divorce and I would have to move out if I wanted to leave because he wouldn't. "Okay, I will," I said and I did. That was May 31, 1981; twenty years almost to the day we were married. I gathered my children around me and told them that their Daddy and I weren't getting along and that we were going to have to live apart. I moved into an apartment.

One morning, a month later, Pio showed up on my doorstep. He wanted to come in. I let him. He embraced me and told me he wanted to make love. "No. No." I said, pushing him away.

He was hurt and angry. "I'm outta here!" He said and left. That was what he always said when he was angry. I let him leave.

He moved into an apartment and I bought the house I am still in, and we both continued to raise our children.

*

The retreat was in Atlanta and so we flew there. Margy took me from my house in my wheelchair. Though I was getting good at walking, I still needed the wheelchair for trips and long distances. Margy and Father One Bun took me on the plane and then brought me to a Catholic Hospital in Atlanta where the retreat was to be held.

I didn't have a clue what to expect. I thought this retreat would be very much like the other Catholic retreats I had gone on before my shooting. The retreat might be something enlightening for a group of like-minded individuals. People would smile and feel like they had personal revelations.

Usually, people left these retreats pumped up but that intensity soon faded. People went back into their real lives afterwards. All these good things they had learned about — saints and goodness and prayer and what not — didn't last. I expected this would be another retreat just like those others.

Inside the hospital was a medium sized amphitheater, mainly used for medical classes. Father One Bun, Margie Ruli and I walked into the crowded amphitheater, looking over the crowd. Half of the people appeared to be nuns and priests. We found our seats and then an announcer said to turn off all recording devices. Apparently, Father de Mello was quite famous and people were ready to write a book about his ideas. Many people stood up and put their recorders outside in the hall.

When everyone was seated again, an averaged-sized Indian man dressed in a sports shirt and slacks came out onto the stage. He stood there alone. There was no music and no mass. Father de Mello, a priest dressed as a laymen, spoke to us all. He had a British accent. "You are all asleep and you may die asleep!" We looked around at each other. What had he said? My eyes widened. What a beginning! What was this man speaking about?

"Did you know that your beliefs are only held by one third of the entire human population? We come from a Judeo—Christian background. Have you ever thought about the other two-thirds of the world?" I hadn't ever really thought about it. I had always just assumed the numbers were different and slanted more in our favor. As he spoke, I realized why he didn't want any tape recorders. Father de Mello was bearing his soul and wanted to create a closeness among the people in the room. "You are all alone in this world and until you are satisfied with that you'll never be happy."

Now at that point, I had been depressed for months and months, maybe almost a year. As I had woken up cognitively, I had felt more and more alienated from everyone. But now, here was a person saying that we all felt this same solitude. We couldn't express it, but we all felt it and in order to go on, we had to accept it. I suddenly felt warmth with everyone in the room. I suddenly felt, for just a moment, at one with the world.

For the first time in my life, I felt free. I had my Master's degree and Pio and I were no longer together. After that workshop, I began to volunteer at hospice. I wanted to work with the sick, the dying and the suffering. The piece of Christianity and Catholicism which remained in me after forty some odd years was still calling on me to suffer.

In hindsight, I really hadn't suffered very much in my life up until then. A few deaths and a sad marriage were the most suffering I could come up with back in 1981. Granted these aren't little things, and, of course, no one ever hopes to qualify one's own or other people's suffering.

America had changed a lot in my life. Everything had been reexamined. All those repressed seeds had come to fruition. The chickens had come home to roost. The seeds had lifted full grown out of the soil as new life on the American landscape, presenting us with new possibilities and problems.

Many women, like myself, had eventually embraced feminism. It freed us. Feminism was ultimately a version of Civil Rights, and equal rights for all people was one of the most important concepts to come out of the 1960s.

Yet with our collective examination of America, we Americans had lost our morality. Our morality pre-1960 had been wound up in believing in patriarchy, segregation, "a woman's place was in the home," strict education, and Christianity. Our moral structure was a joke, a lie.

In 1960, Daddy was fifty years old with five kids, had his own corporation, an elevated position in his community and respect from all. But beyond that façade was a skirt-chasing alcoholic. According to me, he didn't much care about his children and he didn't care about his grandchildren either.

My generation realized the morality represented by our parents was often a lie. We tore down the moral code of our society because we saw its flaws and its collusion with segregation and patriarchy. Yet, we couldn't rebuild anything in its place since the most awake ones of us realized the only moral code a human could create for him or herself was that code which came naturally from within.

Unfortunately, most people are not awake enough to develop their own mores. And so, in place of a new social moral code, we became lenient with our children. Purposefully, we didn't treat them the same way our parents had treated us and in the end we lost our children. The structure of society which remained after the 1960s and 70s was materialism and it was materialism with which we began to raise our children.

Drug use became a hip craze instead of a key to opening one's mind. Music became corporate. Everything became corporate and children chased that and the money filled their eyes and lives. Our children grew up like this. Now they are adults. I sense maybe the pendulum has started to go back, to go back to a healthy place but I don't know.

Today, we seem to be stuck between two positions. One of inner growth and spiritual development and the other of addiction. Humanity has probably always been involved with this dilemma but never to this extent.

For a few years after my divorce, I was living my life freely. I had a life with Larry, my new boyfriend. I worked and met new people. Still, I was continually bothered by my internal need for a sufferer's life. And then on that one fateful day, as I ran in the park, once again, I asked Jesus to shit on me.

That very evening, two young African—American males were
looking for trouble in the Uptown section. They saw a white
woman with blond hair getting out of her car. They hid behind
a tree. The car was a Mercedes so they thought she had money
on her. They thought money would fill their needs. Quietly, they
snuck up behind the woman. They wanted the money in her purse.
They didn't get it right away.

*

The days of the retreat went by without ever having a mass. We
would just meet and Father de Mello would speak to us. He told
us, "Ninety-nine percent of you are afraid of death and you will die
afraid." I listened closely. It seemed to me that death he was right
... fear of death was the great fear and one of our greatest human
problems was denying death. I wanted to cheer when I heard it,
hug him and tell him his words had set me free!

*

Their bullet cut through the air and entered my nose and pushed
cartridge and bone aside. It cut the optic nerve and twisted my left
eye but miraculously didn't kill me. Somehow, it just lodged itself
in the back of my brain where it will stay for the rest of my life.
But in that millisecond, half of all my senses and cognitive abilities
and understanding disappeared. And then the stroke hit. My ears
beeped. My head rang. I was no longer living free. In an instant, I
had became dependent on everyone in my world.

*

I can't give a logical reason for the epiphany I had with Father de
Mello. But I knew it was the truth I had kept hidden in my soul
since childhood! I knew that no organized religion had led me to
recognize that truth, my truth! My fear of death was based on my

need for security and my ego's need for suffering was based on using suffering as a way of avoiding death! I had come so close to death. And the suffering was so extreme! And still nothing was different. Nothing. Nothing.

I knew not what I was but I knew what I was not. I was not Catholic anymore. I didn't know what to believe, but at least I knew that I believed in a power greater than I.

TRANSFORMATION

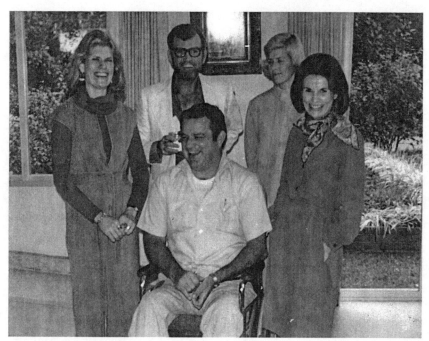

Ruby with family

Ruby at Loyola

Ruby after shooting

Chapter 10

In the summer of 1950, we were vacationing at our ranch outside of Beaumont. Daddy and Momma had some of their friends over and we were all playing Charades. When it was Daddy's turn, he showed us that his answer was going to be six words. Then, suddenly, standing there in front of us all, he made like he was a crucified Jesus on the cross. We all shouted, "Jesus!"

He laughed and made the symbol for two small words. It took us a few minutes but we finally got that he wanted us to finish the sentence, "Jesus was a ... ." Finally, Daddy raised his head up appearing proud, standing tall like General Washington crossing the Potomac. Someone shouted out, "... Fine man!"

We were all a little dumbfounded, "Jesus was a (blank) fine man"? What did this mean? What was the last word?

Then Momma called out, "Jesus was a DAMN fine man!"

Daddy nodded. Some of us laughed. Not everyone thought it was funny though. I remember thinking it was hilarious.

Later, I forgot all about that Texan evening. The shooting however brought back the memory.

I don't know if Daddy believed that Jesus had only been a man but after seeing Father de Mello, I realized that there was no other way for me to think of Jesus. Jesus had definitely been more evolved than most people but ultimately, according to Daddy, he was just "a damn fine man."

*

When I came back from seeing Father de Mello, I told my children that they no longer had to go to mass. I wasn't going to go anymore either. The fact is I had no idea what I believed, or even what was right for me. All I knew was that I believed in a power greater than I.

Now that I look back on it, I can see this was the beginning of my being truly wise. It is amazing for me that we can be wise without being smart. But disabled people like me do it everyday.

I began to read everything I could about Father de Mello. Mentally, I would get the gist of his meaning but I couldn't fully grasp why de Mello's message touched me. All I knew was that I sensed a deep truth about de Mello's writings. The unknown, which de Mello described, was very different from traditional Catholicism. I was in schism from the church. There was no turning back.

After being in the midst of a spiritual crisis for so long, it was calming to now be on a new path which wasn't really a path; but part of a belief system which held no belief. In many ways, this reminded me of Zen where I was totally free. I realized we all were totally free. The fact that everyone was alone meant that we were all together in a very different, deep way. Every day was becoming a kind of passion. I would wake and everyday was like a white canvas I could paint on.

Father de Mello said that we had to understand death, and that only by living with the prospect of our death all the time could we truly realize our life. Bits of discovery would flow through me all day long. As de Mello said, "Reality is always with us, flowing with us, but we break that reality by using words."

How could this shooting have happened to me? Me? It was hard to believe that I had a bullet in my brain. Could I have avoided being shot? There were many "what ifs" in my mind. What if Pio and I had never divorced? Or what if the night I was shot, I had instead stayed with Larry? No one knows. Now, when I look at these possibilities I realize none of them would have mattered. We have a path, there are things which are unavoidable. We can put out energy to influence the thing which will happen to us but ultimately certain events are unavoidable in life.

There were a million different possibilities for how my world could have turned out for me. I had broken from Catholicism but I still hadn't learned about reincarnation so everything seemed very random. There were a myriad of possibilities opening to me.

I wondered why I had been born a woman, when men were the ones with so much power. Why had the police never caught those young men who had shot me? Why had they shot me?

I wanted to think they were on drugs and needed to get high again with my money. I wanted to think that they didn't really know what they had done. I wanted to think that they were just confused adolescents, the same way I had been twenty-five years earlier. I wanted to see them as human beings.

My growing anger at them began to be uncomfortable for me. I would get mad at little insignificant things. My children got the brunt of it. When I was angry, I couldn't talk right! I would start laughing and then crying and I never knew what emotion was coming next. I don't think my poor kids did either. When emotions would fly inside me and I would start laughing, I would say to whomever, "Don't mind me. I'm really angry." And then I would start crying and laughing together. I was all jumbled up.

Psychologically, what was happening to me was entirely new.

As I've written, right after the shooting, I was emotionally blank. Like a gray flat line, I didn't feel anything. Now emotions were coming hard and fast. I didn't know what to expect. I could cry. Then laugh and then be angry about every small thing around me. I could feel again. Now, finally I had some responsibility for my emotions and myself. This was progress! I was in a very difficult psychological place and I knew it was my responsibility to get help. I had to go back to Anne Teachworth. I had to work with her again.

*

Mary Jane didn't see any harm in my learning how to drive again. Though neither one of us thought of me driving alone on my own, we both felt it would be great for me to get back behind the wheel and drive again. Mary Jane was only free to teach me on Sunday mornings so we went to an empty shopping center parking lot near my house and began to drive around the parking lot. Driving was odd because it required my left foot and hand to do everything.

Mary Jane got a necking-knob put on the wheel so it was easier for me to drive with my one hand.

By mid-1986, it had been three years since the shooting. After a few months, I was getting pretty good at driving again.

I could see normally when I drove except for the permanent loss of my right peripheral vision. I was always looking to the right side.

More and more as I was relearning to drive with Mary Jane, I realized if could get around on my own, I could drive out to Metairie and go back to see my old therapist, Anne Teachworth. I had been nervous about doing it before because I didn't want to have to use a cab to get around.

Calling a taxi cab was difficult because speaking on the phone was almost impossible for me. Once in the cab, calculating how much the tip should be was extremely confusing. Since it was difficult for me to speak (extra hard with strangers), I didn't know what to do when I got in a cab.

This whole situation was solved the day I went to get my state I.D. My old driver's license from before the shooting was quite expired. In my present condition, I still didn't think I could drive and I doubted anyone would ever give me my license back. I thought it was best to get a Louisiana state I.D.

Peggy sent me my birth certificate from Beaumont and Mary Jane came over one day to take me to the DMV, Division of Motor Vehicles. As I left the house, I remembered about my old license. I thought it might be easier to get my Louisiana state I.D. if I had my old driving license.

At the DMV. I gave all my documentation to a clerk at the counter. While she was looking at my documents I handed her my old license asking, "Would this help?" She looked at the license and smiled saying, "Yeah, sure. We can give you a new one right now."

"A new one"? What did that mean? They took a new picture of me and put it on a new driver's license without being tested or anything. I was able to drive again.

Both Mary Jane and I felt that it if was OK with the state for me to drive, then I could drive and so I started again. It was wonderful to be able to go all around the city. I never drove on the big interstates but I was easily able to get around on the city roads. It was such a freeing experience. I could go wherever I pleased, whenever I pleased.

Now that I could drive, I was able to comfortably schedule therapy sessions with Anne Teachworth at her office in the suburbs and did. I felt like I belonged in Anne Teachworth's therapy sessions. I felt comfortable. I felt at home. I was placed in a group therapy session. There were about four or five of us in the group.

I continued to have trouble speaking. Sometimes I couldn't fully express myself but Anne was always there to help me get the words out correctly. When I stumbled on a word, Anne would ask me if I was trying to say such-and-such. I would nod "Yes" or shake my head "No." Slowly, we got out the meaning of what I wanted to say. I felt connected to Anne and everyone else in the group. Little by little, I grew to trust that space and the people in it.

If I couldn't say something or if I was angry about something, I would say "Shoot!" I didn't realize I said "Shoot" a lot. I hadn't said shoot that much before the shooting. Anne began to pick up on my using that word and other words which she believed I was using to express my buried emotions regarding the shooting. She said that I needed to deal with the deeper psychological emotions under the words but that I never would if I continued to dismiss them subconsciously with off-handed speech.

Anne stopped me from saying words like, "Shoot!" and "That kills me" or "That slays me." Any careless phrases words to do with murder or death were forbidden for me to say in an off-hand way. She and the rest of the group forced me to take the shooting and the concept of death seriously.

I kept going to Anne Teachworth and I kept driving. The years went by. My rehabilitation continued. I got better at speaking and everything else. I became more conscious. Although, I loved driving and the feeling of freedom it gave me, I must be honest about something. I probably shouldn't have been driving in the first place. It was dangerous for me to be driving. I was very careful but all the same I had gotten my license too easily. In New Orleans, the law is a fluid thing. If a bureaucrat is in a good mood, as most likely the DMV employee was when I went to get my Louisiana state ID, then you get your license instead. In this way, New Orleans is like a Third World country.

Simply put, I had no right peripheral vision in either eye. Even though I looked hard, I still couldn't see everything. Yet the freedom of being able to drive was additive. When I felt low or wanted to escape from my life, I imagined I just needed to get on the road and go to Beaumont or Colorado or somewhere else. Thankfully I never left town. Leaving doesn't work. The world and our problems follow us wherever we go. By then, I knew I can't escape reality. Naturally, I had a few fender benders but I kept on driving. I liked the freedom.

It took me three years to really open up in Anne's therapy group before I could release the anger I had kept buried inside my mind. Much of those early years were filled with my physical rehabilitation. Recovering from PTSD was even harder. Post-Traumatic Stress Disorder produces denial, avoidance of repressed feelings and terrorizing flashbacks which made me feel the shooting was happening all over again. Gradually, I was getting to feel safe and emotionally comfortable in the group. I had to let them be my support system.

During those three years, both my Momma and Daddy died.

Daddy went first. He had smoked all his life and by 1987, he carried a respirator around with him all the time. He had heart trouble for years and finally he had a bad heart attack that killed him. I don't remember much of Daddy in his last years. We had really grown apart. Even before my shooting, we were distant with each other.

Momma died a year later in 1988 from congestive heart failure. It happened right after I had cosmetic surgery to straighten my left eye. I got the bandage off my eye and was planning on taking a train to Beaumont to see Momma when I heard from Peggy that Momma had taken ill and had gone into the hospital. None of us thought that she would die. I figured that she would be out of the hospital in a few days.

Peggy told Mary and me a story about Momma dying. Peggy was in the hospital room alone with Momma and Momma was very sick. Momma said that she wanted to die, that she had lost so much, and so many people she loved. Momma said she was ready but that she was afraid of dying. Peggy said that being afraid of death was normal. She held Momma's hand for a long time. Then Peggy had to leave the room for a moment and a nurse came in to watch Momma. When Peggy came back in she learned from the nurse that Momma had passed on while she had been away.

At the end of her life, Momma thought she had been a failure. She felt low about herself. Like many women of her generation, Momma hadn't had much self esteem to start with. I don't agree with Momma about her life. For me, her life was a triumph. She had overcome so many losses. By the time she died, had already buried four of her seven children and death with the tragedy of my being shot.

Momma had always been a brave solider, always going on with her steely discipline, just the way she had told us to be. She had a Catholic way of looking at death, everything in life was a trial. According to me, this may not have been a healthy way to deal with death but she forged on. With all of her repressions, and she had them, Momma was the rock that we kids built ourselves around.

I remember one time after I was shot, I went to Beaumont with Mary Jane. Momma came out and greeted me at her house and we embraced each other and cried. She looked at me and said, "Sometimes I wonder what it's all about?" She said hadn't been to mass in 2 or 3 weeks. This was after I had left the church. All I could say was, "I don't know Momma." And I didn't know. I guess I don't know. Not even today, I don't.

Any psychologist could easily see why I had PTSD from almost dying from a bullet to my head that was still lodged in my brain.

Finally by 1989, I was ready to deal with myself psychologically. By 1989, I had gotten to a cognitive and physical place where I could express myself. But it would never have happened had I not met one young woman named Elizabeth.

Elizabeth joined Anne's group therapy session in 1989. If there was a new person in our group therapy session, we always introduced ourselves and explained why we were in the session. On Elizabeth's first day, we all went around and when it was my turn to speak I said, "I'm here to get over being shot in the head six years ago."

Elizabeth had a strange look on her face after I spoke.

Anne noticed and asked her, "Elizabeth, do you want to say something about what Ruby had said?" Elizabeth told a story about a good friend of hers who had been shot and killed. Her story touched something off inside of me. Something was unlocked.

It was like Elizabeth could somehow share my experience. I was opening up. I began to speak about how I felt about the shooting. I spoke about my anger, and I felt the feeling of anger rising inside of me. Suddenly, all of the strange emotions I had been feeling since the shooting jelled together. I understood why I was angry. I understood why I cried so much. It was another epiphany for me.

Man, was I angry! Fatherfuck, I was so angry! I didn't give a damn about any explanation for this. Those young men had been born into poverty? They were on drugs? Really? Well, I didn't give a damn anymore! I had no compassion or understanding for them like I was thinking I should have,

How dare they do this to me and take half of me away! May they be damned so some kind of eternal hell, I thought.

I sat up in my chair, furious, no longer the seemingly nice, polite Texan woman I had been before when I talked about the shooting. As I spoke to the group, I realized that my external façade had been just that; a lie. I was livid. I had a right to be. For the first time in my life, I had a right to be angry.

I began crying a lot because nice Southern Christian women like me have a problem with being angry. Instead of getting angry, they end up crying. Anne didn't let anyone console me or try to get me to stop crying. She even stopped anyone from offering me a Kleenex because she said that was "stop crying" behavior. She said that I had to be left alone with my tears and my anger. It was up to me. After the crying passed, we began as a group to deal with my emotions.

We got feedback from everyone in the group. I felt like some of the people in the group were emotionally connected with me and how I was feeling and some weren't. They just listened. But life is like that, isn't it? So at the end of each session, we all hugged each other since they had all been there together for me to re-experience the feelings from my trauma in this safe place.

The process of diffusing my Post Traumatic Stress took many sessions. During this period, our group would have a normal session where everyone spoke about their issues and then I would talk at the end of each session.

After dealing with my initial anger, Anne had me do a corrective emotional experience. She asked me what would I do if I could do whatever I wanted to the teenagers who had shot me. She took two pillows and put them in front of me. "Ruby, I want you to pretend that these pillows are your two attackers. What would you like to do to them?" she asked. Gladly, I told the group what I would do to the young men.

Then, using the two pillows as stand-ins for the two men, Anne asked me to pretend I was actually doing it to them. To start with, I only yelled and cursed at them but that wasn't enough for me. I wanted more. They had to suffer. So I began to torture them. The torture went on for several sessions.

At the end of each group, I would hit the young men (i.e. pillows) with my cane saying, "Take that, FATHER fuckers!" I loved to beat them and beat them. I beat them until I couldn't raise my good arm anymore. Then I said to them, "I'm gonna give you hospital beds to live in, even though you didn't give me a hospital bed, I'm gonna give each of y'all one!"

Then I'd imagine I'd go visit them in the hospital and beat them in their beds. I gave them each an eye patch to use for their left eyes. I made sure their right sides were paralyzed. Everything was just like what had happened to me. Then I made them use a wheelchair to get around. When they walked they had to hold their butts in just like I still had to. I loved it.

One session, I shot them both in the face. I didn't have any plans for it to happen that afternoon. It was already late in the session and it was my weekly turn to beat my robbers. All of a sudden, that wasn't good enough. The urge to shoot them just came over me like it must have just come over the one who shot me years ago. In the middle of beating them hard with my cane, I yelled out, "Aw, fuck it. I'm just gonna shoot you, Fatherfuckers!"

And I did. Without a moment of hesitation, I shot both of them in the nose and gave both of them the same brain injury and same pain I had experienced. I lodged a bullet in each brain and they were forced to live with it there like I am. Finally satisfied, I stopped. I lowered my left hand which I had used as the gun to shoot the teenagers.

It may seem complicated but I felt complete relief for doing to them what was done to me. The therapy exercise was sort of a reverse Golden Rule. Instantly, my anger ebbed away. I was tranquil. I could hear the other group therapy members clapping for me. I was elated. It was like running! A lot of that that built up anger-receded. Even though, the anger would never completely leave me, now I no longer repress it. Instead, now that I can understand I am entitled to feel it, I can choose to leave it aside.

I wonder now what would have happened if I had not had therapy. Would I have continued to be angry suddenly for no reason? Or would I have continued to be a polite, demure and squelched woman? Probably, I would have been a little of all of these negative facades and outcomes put together. But with the help of a good therapist, I was able to learn a lot about myself, have the courage to confront my anger at my robbers and my fear of being angry at them, too.

Everyone from our group was around me cheering now. They were all hugging me and each other. I had done it! I had gone through my anger and come out on the other side.

Chapter 11

I continued to go to Anne Teachworth for a few years. Among other things, we worked on some of my other repressed feelings, ones about my family, my parents, society, patriarchy and organized religion.

After going through my anger over the shooting, I found that I was able to deal with these other emotional avoidances in a new way. I know it is sometimes scary but I strongly believe that if you have psychological issues you ought to seek the help of a good therapist. A good therapist, one who works with you and who you like, is invaluable. Even if it takes time to find the right therapist (you may have to try a few different ones), it is worth it.

One day after group therapy, I was leaving the office with my hand on the door knob when Anne called me over to her. She told me that she wanted me to come to her office the next day, a Saturday. "Aw, Anne," I said, "On Saturday? My one day to sleep in?"

"I know that," she said, "but I want you to come here anyway. I'm going to have a very special person here for you to meet. His name is Ron Hall." So on Saturday I hot footed it down to Anne's office to see this speaker. Who was this Ron Hall person? Anne said Ron was a very important therapist. It turned out Ron was a lot more than a therapist.

Ron was standing outside Anne's house when I drove up there that day. Back then, Anne lived in Uptown New Orleans in a beautiful condominium on St. Charles Avenue. Ron was on the grass in front yard looking at the sun and the trees and the flowers. I got out of my car and walked over to him. "You must be Ron Hall," I said. "I'm Ruby Lyons."

We shook hands and he invited me to go inside of Anne's house/ office for his talk. As I talked to him out in the yard, Ron reminded me of Ranny. They had the same mannerisms, the same hand gestures, Ron had a beard like Ranny and seemed as easy going as Ranny had been.

I went inside and saw Anne. Around her, were ten people already seated for Ron's workshop. We were in the same room where I normally had my group therapy sessions. There was a massage table set up in the front of the room. On it, were what looked like "rocks," at least to my Texan eyes, that is what they were. Later, I found out that these were crystals and that they had special healing powers. Ron described what he did with clients as Awakenings.

Ron spoke to us about energy, auras and psychology and then we had a coffee break. We all followed Ron to the kitchen. During a lull in the conversation, I said, "Ron, I was shot in the head." Obviously surprised, he responded, "Oh you were! I was shot, too."

He described the day he was shot in the stomach. Seems Ron was part-owner of a record store in the 70s. One day, a man came in and without any hesitation, pulled out a gun, shooting Ron in the hand. The man demanded money from the register and Ron gave it to him. The robber left. Then Ron had the nerve to chase the man down the street, and he turned around and shot Ron in the stomach.

Ron managed to make it to a house, told the owner to call 911, and passed out. Luckily, the bullet didn't hit any of Ron's other major organs. After a few surgeries, Ron had returned to his normal self carrying the scars on his hand and stomach.

When I learned that Ron had also been shot, I felt a kinship with him. I feel this same bond for anyone who is shot.

Anyway, we went back to the workshop and Ron continued his talk. Much of what he said sounded as if it came directly from Father de Mello. I guess Ron's sounding like de Mello isn't strange. Awareness and Awakening are the same experience no matter what culture you come from. I knew I wanted to see Ron again. I whispered to Anne that I wanted to see Ron privately for a session.

When I think about Ron now, I smile. I've said before that he reminded me of Ranny. I felt right at home with Ron right away. When he told me that he had been shot, I felt a particular bond with him. I had never met anyone else who had lived through being shot.

When we met again, Ron greeted me and took me to a small room in Anne Teachworth's office. In the room, there was a desk and his massage table in it. On the massage table, once again, were some crystals. He also had a big box of Crayolas. "Ruby," Ron said, "I want you to draw anything you feel like drawing. Anything at all." And he left the room.

I sat down and looked at the paper. At first, I drew the sun and then I drew the front porch of my lavender-colored house on Webster Street. Next to my house, I drew my five children as stick figures, all in red. After about five minutes, Ron knocked and asked if he could come in and look at my picture. First, he analyzed the sun. He said that this was a good sign. Then he looked at my house and said there was something about the color of lavender which was good. Finally, Ron got to my children. "I see a little bit of anger there," he told me.

Red is the color of anger, he said. I told him that I did wish my children were closer to me, that they understood me better. Ron said, "All of our anger comes from our wishes, our desires. Some day, you'll reconnect with them, with all of them." Ron knew just how to ask questions to make a person eager to answer, learn and go deeper into him or herself. Our conversation flowed easily.

I was so relaxed and comfortable with Ron. When I told him more about being shot, I began to cry. Ron looked at me very quizzically and said, "Ruby, what you did was shot yourself."

Without a pause, I asked, "Ron, do you believe in reincarnation?" He looked shocked that I would ask such a question. I was shocked, too, that I had asked that. "Of course." he said, as if there was no other way to believe.

As usual, I started reading everything I could about reincarnation. I write "as usual" because you probably can tell by now that if I am doing something, I do it full force.

First I read the book, "Many Lives, Many Mansions." It was written by a psychiatrist named Dr. Brian Wiess who believed in traditional psychiatric practices until he began treating a patient who while under hypnosis, seemed to slip into other personalities from the past. While in trance, the patient was also able to speak other languages which she had never learned.

Because of this clinical evidence, Dr. Wiess began to move away from traditional psychology and into the realm of metaphysical psychology, and began to incorporate reincarnation into his practice. I began reading all kinds of esoteric texts. I was interested in how Eastern and Western cultures came together. I was open, for the first time, to an entirely different spirituality. To only be in this one body for a moment in eternity and then to pass on and have my soul go into another body, gave me new answers to questions I had been asking since I was a little girl.

I had left aside my Catholicism years earlier, believing only in a "power" greater than I. I sensed this power was both male and female in my understanding of it but really the power itself was genderless. The power transcended gender and became one energy.

After reincarnation came into my life, this idea of a Godless God/Goddess became fully formed in my mind. The church had never really fulfilled me but interestingly enough, there was a long tradition (buried and repressed now) of reincarnation within Western religious tradition. In fact, the Catholic Church had once persecuted 12th Century Christian Gnostics who lived in the Mediterranean region because they believed in reincarnation.

In my studies, I came across an amazing woman named Caroline Myss who had combined the Eastern and Western thought. She is called a medical Intuitive in the alternative medical world.

Just by talking to a doctor (and not seeing the patient), Caroline could tell the doctor exactly what medical condition was ailing the patient. The doctor could then apply the appropriate medical care to the patient. Caroline had discovered her intuition by studying the Indian Chakras and at the same time, studying traditional Western Medicine.

Reincarnation explained to me why I had been shot. Ron opened the door for me and as I studied reincarnation, I crossed the threshold into a new life. I no longer had to blame someone for shooting me. I came to realize that somehow I might have done the same thing to someone else at some time in the past. It was called "karma." Reincarnation allowed me to know that my shooting was the evolutionary and energetic response to what I had done before (i.e. shoot someone). I know my belief might seem a little morbid and a lot of people would deny my conclusions about my shooting, but it makes sense to me.

We can sit and debate personal volition vs. fatalism, and we can talk about God sitting mighty and masculine on His throne meting out His justice, or we can talk about the truth that God and the Goddess are one and we are all the one God/Goddess who lives in us and we in Him/Her. Or we can argue this stuff. But obviously, Fatherfuck, I believe I am right when I tell you that you are the Goddess, and I am too.

But you might not arrive at my understanding. It takes an old soul to get to where I am now. I know this realization took me centuries. I know I went through many lives to get to this in me. I don't remember the lives but I know that I was evolving and not evolving at the same moment. I was transforming, always.

And I know that Time doesn't exist. I also know that Death is with us from the moment we are born.

There is a duality of progress and being complete in the same moment. There is a duality of death and life. There is and there isn't. Ultimately, what we have are mysteries all around us and in us. The point isn't to look for answers. I'm not sure what the point is, but I feel a peace by understanding the world with reincarnation. Reincarnation has been the belief which has rebuilt my world.

Ron called himself an Awakener. He would give talks about spirituality and then he would take individuals who wanted private sessions. In the private sessions, Ron would psychologically examine a person and "wake a person up."

Of course, everything was up to the person. Ron didn't force anything; he just said what he thought was true for that person.

Ron was from Georgia. I went once to his home there in the countryside. He traveled all over the world giving talks and doing Awakenings. Though Ron did ask for donations for this work, he was by no means rich. People just respected his abilities and paid a fair fee for his help. Interestingly, most of Ron's clients were women. Does this mean that we women are more in tune to our spirituality? Well, I don't know. I believe that men generally have a masculinity which keeps them closed up.

Ron himself was masculine, and no one would have guessed when they first met him but he was gay. Normally Ron's sexual orientation wouldn't be important enough to include in my writing but I find it interesting that in many cultures homosexual people are the shamans and spiritual leaders. As far as I've read, a good number of Native American tribes had homosexual shamans. In Western culture, the Catholic church's clergy — both male and female — have been predominantly homosexual since the church's inception.

When Ron first came to New Orleans, he would give his Awakenings and talks at Anne's house/office. I always wanted to see Ron when he was in town. As I grew more into life with reincarnation, Ron and I had many conversations. He became a good friend. Around about this time, in the early 1990s, I began to have the idea of writing my story. I half-joked with Ron that he would be the star in the book. I write "half-joked" because Ron laughed when I told him that he would be the main character in my book, "I'll just be mentioned, Ruby. Maybe I'll have a little part but that is all." He was right. I guess I'm the star of my book.

Ron also held retreats with other Awakeners. Usually a retreat was held one weekend a year. They were generally in South Carolina, Georgia or Louisiana at country homes or inns.

I remember the first retreat I went to. It was at a country home in Northern Louisiana, outside of a town called Alexandria. I took a bus up to Alexandria and felt very scared. I was alone. I had no idea how this new retreat would go. I was met at the bus station by a woman named Susan who was very kind. Susan drove me to the retreat and stayed in a guest house with me.

None of my fears were warranted. Usually fears are never warranted. The people at the retreat were very open and warm. Even though everyone except Ron was new to me, it was as if I had known them for many years. I think I was touching on the piece

of reincarnation that teaches a human soul knows its path before it
enters a new body. It knows what will happen in this new life but
then the moment it enters the body, the soul forgets all of
that knowledge.

So at heart, I already knew all these people at the retreat and they
knew me. We'd known each other for ages but we had just forgotten
who we were to each other. Ron and the other awakeners helped us
remember. They used crystals for energy. We lay on our backs and
the Awakeners would move crystals above our bodies. Now, I know
that many of you might find ideas like crystals and energy "a little
out there." But it is just like what I wrote about reincarnation. It
worked for me and it still does. The use of energy and crystals gave
me a more complete understanding of life.

I have truly gained tranquility towards life since my shooting. I
have lived and learned so much since the shooting that I doubt I
would have evolved to this point had I not been shot. If I had it to
do over again, I would not choose to be shot, of course. I would
have chosen to not ask Jesus to "shit on me." But my being shot
is the thing which pushed me toward this new unknown horizon.
Would I have gotten here without the shooting? Who knows and
who cares? Questions like this are really just egotism. There is
no growth in these kinds of questions. Basically I am where I am
meant to be.

In 1991, Anne Teachworth moved her practice from Uptown New
Orleans to Metairie, a suburb of New Orleans. I realized it would be
hard for Ron's clients to go all the way out to Anne's new practice
so I wrote Ron a Christmas card and in it explained that if he
wanted to, he was welcome to do his Awakenings in my home. Ron
called me and told me that he would love to work out of my house.

And so it was set. Ron was to visit and stay with me whenever he came to New Orleans.

We grew even closer when he was staying at my house. Ron and his clients encouraged me to start to do my own Awakenings. But I thought better of it. I would have felt awkward had I done Awakening sessions. I was too shy to do them. But Ron's visiting gave me a real opportunity to ask Ron all kinds of questions about Awakening and reincarnation. Ron was the law of attraction put in to practice. The law of attraction states that you get back the energy that you put out.

Ron never had an unkind word to say about anyone anywhere on their journey. He was always loving towards everyone. He explained that we all have our own "guidance" and that voice inside of us, if we cultivate it, will never let us down. The guidance is different from ego. If we listen to our "guidance," we will always be right. We can't go astray on our own path.

Right before his death in April 2005, Ron began telling people that a major hurricane and flood were coming to New Orleans. He thought it would be the next year, in 2006. He was off by a year. Ron said many people would not want to return here because of the toxic waters. He felt bad about this because he had so many friends and loved ones living in New Orleans.

In April 2005, when he was only fifty-six years old, Ron got a tooth abscess. He went to the dentist who gave him some antibiotics. The antibiotics worked against his body and soon he had hematoma all over. He went back to the doctor and the doctor gave him a different type of antibiotic. The hematoma went away but Ron was still very ill. He forced himself to do a scheduled retreat at a friend's house. At the retreat, he said he could no longer hear his "guidance." This was shocking to some of the people at the retreat who knew Ron well.

After the retreat, Ron insisted on driving home alone that night. The next day, he awoke ill and to decided to take a cab to the doctor. On the ride to the hospital, he leaned over and died. I was in shock when I heard Ron had left us. It took over a week for the realization of his death to sink in. So we planned a FUN-ural for him. I say "FUN" because that is how some of us in New Orleans celebrate death. In New Orleans we like to say, we put the FUN back in funeral, with parades and processions and music New Orleanians like to celebrate death.

Those of us who had known and loved Ron didn't have a Jazz Funeral for him but we did all meet and talk about Ron and have a party. It was a dichotomy. Ron's funeral was joyous and sad at the same time. We were sad for his loss yet happy for his life and where he was now.

*

Ever since the shooting, I have feared falling. It is the most basic fear I know. To fall, means to be helpless. And being helpless brings everything back. In the past twenty-five years since the shooting, I have fallen many times. But only once was I injured. Once was enough.

In January 2002, I was leaving a clothing store. The women's section was on the second floor. Before going up the stairs, I made sure that there was a railing on both sides to hold. As I was leaving the store, I walked back down the stairway. I didn't realize there wasn't a bottom step on the stairway and I stepped too far and fell face down on the floor and knocked over a rack of ties. I managed to turn over and with my left hand, reached down to the floor pushing myself up. But in my head, my left arm and my left fingers, there began a constant pain so strong I couldn't move. I lay on the ground hurting so much that I began to cry. I cried dry tears.

By the way, there are two kinds of tears. One is weeping sad tears. The other kind is when you hurt so badly that nothing comes out. You just moan. So I was crying/moaning. A male employee held my hand as I lay there on the floor. I told him to call the ambulance and then to call my son who was a doctor.

It seems like I waited forever for the ambulance to arrive. It kept missing the store. I watched the ambulance pass two or three times before finally stopping in front of the store.

The attendants put me in a neck brace. Then they loaded me into the ambulance. The driver said he would go very slowly because he knew the bumps in the street hurt my head and shoulder. We got to the hospital. My eldest son was there with a few other doctors. They took x-rays of my shoulder and then gave me a temporary sling to wear and a prescription for pain killers. I went home.

All of my children heard about my fall. My youngest son had just arrived back in the States from working in Central America. He took it upon himself to care for me. I don't know what I would have done without him. I couldn't do anything! I couldn't go to the bathroom, I couldn't eat, I couldn't bathe. Nothing. I was reminded of Baptist Hospital back in 1983 and how helpless I was there. But this time, I was conscious of everything, all the pain and all of the decisions I'd made to get here.

About a week after the fall, my youngest son and caregiver took me to see my oldest son. Flanked by x-rays in his office, my oldest son explained to me that I had two options. One, I could do nothing and my shoulder would heal but I would only be able to raise my only good arm shoulder height. Or two, a surgery could be performed whereby I would regain full motion of my left arm. Orthopedically, a small chip of bone in my left shoulder had broken off and I needed it removed.

So the choice was up to me. I decided on the surgery. My son warned me that it would be a long healing process. But I wanted full use of my one remaining arm (my right side has never fully come back from the stroke, yet). The surgery went by very smoothly. There was no pain until after the surgery. It was excruciating. From my shoulder down to my finger tips, pain flowed. It was one continuous ache.

My youngest son kept pushing the button for the nurse to come and give me pain killers. But she never did. He went out in the hall and yelled at the nurses. Eventually, they brought in morphine and gave it to me intravenously.

It was a slow road to recovery. My youngest son was with me for the whole time. He fed me, cleaned me and put me on my bed pan. He organized caretakers to come and give him small breaks when he needed it but otherwise he was always there.

The second rehabilitation took less time than my first. Within a year and a half, I was back to normal.

The only trace of the fall were my new seizures. I began having them after the surgery. I had bumped my head when I had fallen and the doctors guessed this had brought on the seizures. It is only recently in 2008 that I have stopped taking the seizure medication.

I want you to know how important it was for me to be fully conscious and feel my trauma for the second time. After my fall in 2002, I was reduced to what I had been in 1983 after being shot. The difference was that I was conscious of everything in 2002. During my second rehabilitation, I was able to review all of what had happened in my life before. But I was able to look at it with a new belief system.

Our life is like an ascending circle which keeps on going. Many times we're stopped and stagnant, sometimes for centuries. In my life, I've seen violence. I think it comes when we are not being awake and aware. Violence comes from fear. There are two extremes in life: fear and love.

We humans selflessly get involved in other people's happiness. And why? Because we selfishly want them to make us happy. Ultimately, our brains want pleasure, not pain, so we create a life around safety and comfort. Yet when suffering rears its ugly head ... we hide like ostriches with our heads in the sand.

As long as we don't look too deeply within ourselves and our society, there will be no transformation to happiness and love. We will simply continue in a state of denial and fear. In order to transform ourselves and society, we have but just to go into our hearts and listen.

In order to transform oneself, we have to go into our hearts and listen. In my heart, I am still running in the park, only this time, I am saying, "Thank you, Goddess, for giving me my life back."

Basic Principles of Life

by Betty Jean Wall
The Power to Heal Myself, 2009

We are love.

We are CONSCIOUSNESS.

We are already enlightened.

We just have to show up and be present.

We are here to serve, to share.

We are joy, laughter, and happiness, FUN.

In addition to nurturing each other with food, we can
nurture each other's souls by being kind, compassionate,
forgiving. We are all reflections of each other.

Books from Gestalt Institute Press

LaVergne, TN USA
07 October 2009
160213LV00002B/4/P